Best of Bridge

Kitchen Simple

125 Quick & Easy Recipes

Robert
ROSE

For complete cataloguing information, see page 240.

Disclaimer
The recipes in this book have been carefully tested by our kitchen and our tasters. To the best of our knowledge, they are safe and nutritious for ordinary use and users. For those people with food or other allergies, or who have special food requirements or health issues, please read the suggested contents of each recipe carefully and determine whether or not they may create a problem for you. All recipes are used at the risk of the consumer.

We cannot be responsible for any hazards, loss or damage that may occur as a result of any recipe use.

For those with special needs, allergies, requirements or health problems, in the event of any doubt, please contact your medical adviser prior to the use of any recipe.

Design and production: Kevin Cockburn/PageWave Graphics Inc.
Editor: Kathleen Fraser
Indexer: Gillian Watts
Photography: Jonathan Bielaski
Food stylist: Andrew Bullis
Prop stylist: Mecayla Slaviero

Cover image: Skillet Chicken and Couscous (page 114)

The publisher gratefully acknowledges the financial support of our publishing program by the Government of Canada through the Canada Book Fund.

Canadä

Published by Robert Rose Inc.
120 Eglinton Avenue East, Suite 800, Toronto, Ontario, Canada M4P 1E2
Tel: (416) 322-6552 Fax: (416) 322-6936
www.robertrose.ca

Printed and bound in China

1 2 3 4 5 6 7 8 9 LEO 29 28 27 26 25 24 23 22 21

CONTENTS

INTRODUCTION

WHAT DOES *KITCHEN SIMPLE* MEAN TO US? LET'S LOOK AT THOSE TWO WORDS.

KITCHEN — OURS, YOURS, A FAMILY KITCHEN WHERE WE COOK MEALS, DO HOMEWORK, MAKE PHONE CALLS, PUT AWAY THE GROCERIES, FEED THE FAMILY PET AND SO MUCH MORE. IT SEEMS AS IF SO MUCH GETS DONE IN THE KITCHEN, SO HOW CAN IT BE SIMPLE?

SIMPLE USUALLY DESCRIBES SOMETHING THAT ISN'T COMPLICATED. SIMPLE MEANS EASY TO UNDERSTAND OR A PROBLEM CAN BE SOLVED EASILY.

COMBINING "SIMPLE" WITH ALL THE THINGS GOING ON IN OUR KITCHENS MAY SEEM LIKE A PARADOX, BUT WE WANT TO HELP YOU KEEP YOUR KITCHEN SIMPLE. NOT THAT WE WANT TO TAKE AWAY ANY OF THE EXCITEMENT FROM WHAT IS HAPPENING IN YOUR KITCHEN, BUT WE JUST DON'T WANT TO COMPLICATE IT. WITH THIS BOOK, WE WANT TO HELP YOU GET DINNER ON THE TABLE WITHOUT A LOT OF FUSS OR COMPLICATED METHODS OR INGREDIENTS. OUR GOAL IS TO GIVE YOU THE TOOLS TO CREATE WONDERFUL AND FLAVORFUL DISHES AND BE SUPER PROUD AND PLEASED WITH YOUR RESULTS.

WE ARE SO HAPPY TO SEE THAT MANY MORE PEOPLE ARE COOKING AT HOME AND WE HOPE THAT ENTHUSIASM CONTINUES TO INCREASE. MANY HOME COOKS ARE NEW TO THE KITCHEN, OR THEY ARE TAKING TIME TO SHARE FAMILY RECIPES AND COOKING SKILLS WITH YOUNGER FAMILY MEMBERS OR LEARNING TOGETHER ALONGSIDE A PARTNER. WE KNOW THAT GOOD FOOD DOES NOT HAVE TO BE COMPLICATED.

NO MATTER WHETHER YOU ARE JUST STARTING OUT OR YOU ARE AN EXPERIENCED COOK, OUR RECIPES WILL OFFER YOU SIMPLE TECHNIQUES AND INGREDIENTS TO CREATE AN ABUNDANCE OF DELICIOUS FLAVOR COMBINATIONS SURE TO WHET APPETITES AND SATISFY HUNGRY FAMILY AND FRIENDS.

SO WHAT MAKES *KITCHEN SIMPLE* DIFFERENT? WE'VE INCLUDED SIMPLE, SMART STRATEGIES AND TECHNIQUES TO STREAMLINE GETTING MEALS ON THE TABLE. THAT MEANS TASTY MEALS EASILY COME TOGETHER USING INGREDIENTS YOU CAN FIND AT THE GROCERY STORE — NO TRIPS TO SPECIALTY STORES — AND WITHOUT SPENDING TOO MUCH TIME IN THE KITCHEN. PLAN WHAT YOU WANT TO MAKE SIMPLY BY PICKING OUT THE RECIPES YOU WANT TO TRY OR THE INGREDIENTS YOU HAVE AT HOME; THEN READ THROUGH THE RECIPE AND YOU ARE READY TO GO. BE SURE TO CHECK OUT OUR TIPS: THEY CAN HELP YOU GET A HEAD-START ON MEAL PREPARATION THE DAY BEFORE OR SAVE TIME (AND DISHES) THE DAY YOU COOK!

WE LOVE TO INCLUDE HELPFUL TIME-SAVERS, LIKE PRECUT FROZEN VEGETABLES, STORE-BOUGHT BOTTLED SAUCES, SPICE MIXES AND FROZEN PASTA. SOME OF OUR RECIPES CREATE SIMPLICITY BY ADOPTING "HANDS-FREE" COOKING TOOLS, LIKE THE INSTANT POT OR USING ONE SKILLET OR A SHEET PAN TO GET DINNER DONE. *KITCHEN SIMPLE* ALSO INCLUDES CLEVER NEW TAKES ON SOME CLASSIC FAVORITES, MAKING THEM LESS WORK IN THE KITCHEN, BUT WITHOUT SACRIFICING TASTE, LIKE SHEET-PAN BUTTERMILK CINNAMON PANCAKES (PAGE 14), SPIRAL PASTA TACO SKILLET SUPPER (PAGE 130),

TURKEY ZUCCHINI MEATBALLS (PAGE 108), NACHO CHIP DIP (PAGE 38) AND SKILLET CHERRY CORNMEAL COBBLER (PAGE 230).

WITH SO MANY DELICIOUS AND EASY RECIPES, HOW DO YOU KNOW WHERE TO START? WELL, WE KNOW THAT WHEN YOU ARE DECIDING WHAT TO MAKE, YOU WILL FACTOR IN PREP TIME, NUMBER OF INGREDIENTS, AND HOW FAR IN ADVANCE IT CAN BE PREPARED, NOT TO MENTION IF YOUR FAMILY WILL EAT IT! WE HAVE GREAT NEWS FOR YOU — WHEN YOU FLIP THROUGH THE RECIPES, YOU'LL NOTICE THAT WE'VE ADDED ICONS TO GUIDE YOU IN YOUR SELECTIONS. WE HOPE THEY HELP YOU TO QUICKLY CHOOSE RECIPES AND NAVIGATE MEAL PLANNING. SEE THE ICON KEY ON THE FOLLOWING PAGE SO YOU KNOW WHAT TO LOOK FOR.

FOOD BRINGS PEOPLE CLOSER, WHETHER YOU'RE COOKING TOGETHER OR SHARING A MEAL. WITH THESE SIMPLE RECIPES AND TIPS IN HAND, IT'S EASY TO BRING FRIENDS AND FAMILY INTO THE KITCHEN TO MAKE DELICIOUS AND FUN MEMORIES. WE HOPE THEY HELP TAKE YOU THERE!

DON'T FORGET TO SHARE YOUR *KITCHEN SIMPLE* JOURNEY. WE LOVE TO SEE WHAT YOU'RE COOKING FROM BEST OF BRIDGE, SO POST YOUR PHOTOS OF YOUR RECIPES YOU'VE CREATED FROM THIS COOKBOOK AND BE SURE TO TAG US ON INSTAGRAM @BESTOFBRIDGE AND ON FACEBOOK. THANKS FOR CONTINUING TO FOLLOW OUR FOOD TRIP IN OUR KITCHENS AND BEYOND.

SIMPLY ENJOY!

—EMILY AND SYLVIA

KEY TO RECIPE ICONS

15 MINUTES OR LESS: RECIPES THAT CAN BE PREPARED FROM START TO FINISH IN 15 MINUTES OR LESS

30 MINUTES OR LESS: RECIPES THAT CAN BE PREPARED FROM START TO FINISH IN 30 MINUTES OR LESS

MAKE AHEAD: RECIPES THAT CAN BE PREPARED IN ADVANCE

5 INGREDIENTS OR FEWER: RECIPES THAT USE 5 MAIN INGREDIENTS OR FEWER (NOT INCLUDING WATER, OILS, SALT AND BLACK PEPPER)

10 INGREDIENTS OR FEWER: RECIPES THAT USE 10 MAIN INGREDIENTS OR FEWER (NOT INCLUDING WATER, OILS, SALT AND BLACK PEPPER)

GRILLING: RECIPES THAT ARE COOKED ON THE BARBEQUE

SHEET PAN: RECIPES THAT ARE COOKED ON A SHEET PAN AND BAKED IN THE OVEN

ONE SKILLET/POT MEAL: RECIPES THAT REQUIRE ONLY ONE POT OR ONE SKILLET TO COOK

HERE ARE A FEW MORE TIPS TO HELP YOU IN YOUR *KITCHEN SIMPLE* JOURNEY:

- IF YOU DON'T HAVE THE CORRECT CAN SIZE, SIMPLY NOTE THE VOLUME OR WEIGHT INCLUDED IN THE RECIPE AND MEASURE OUT WHAT YOU NEED FOR THE RECIPE.

- IF YOU HAVE SOME LEFTOVERS FROM CANNED INGREDIENTS, SUCH AS TOMATO PASTE, TOMATOES OR TOMATO SAUCE, BE SURE TO FIND OTHER RECIPES IN THE BOOK TO USE IT IN OR FREEZE IT FOR ANOTHER TIME.

- IF YOU COOK YOUR OWN BEANS AND LEGUMES INSTEAD OF USING CANNED, YOU WILL NEED 2 CUPS (500 ML) FOR THE 19 OZ/540 ML CAN SIZES. YOU CAN FREEZE LEFTOVER COOKED BEANS AND LEGUMES AND, WHILE YOU'RE AT IT, EVEN RICE! SO COOK SOME UP AND USE IT IN RECIPES THAT CALL FOR COOKED RICE.

- STORE YOUR NUTS AND SEEDS IN THE FREEZER SO YOU HAVE THEM AT THE READY WHEN YOU NEED THEM FOR A RECIPE.

- KEEP A RUNNING LIST OF PANTRY STAPLES ON THE FRIDGE SO ON YOUR NEXT TRIP TO THE GROCERY STORE YOU CAN PICK THEM UP TO ALWAYS HAVE THE INGREDIENTS YOU NEED TO MAKE YOUR *KITCHEN SIMPLE* RECIPES.

- PRE-CHOP VEGGIES THE NIGHT BEFORE, WRAP THEM WELL AND REFRIGERATE SO YOU ARE READY FOR COOKING THE NEXT DAY.

BREAKFAST AND BRUNCH

CREAMY APPLE PIE OATS

THIS PERFECT COMBINATION HAS A WONDERFUL AROMA THAT WILL MAKE YOU THINK OF A HOT APPLE PIE IN THE MORNING. IT'S OLD-SCHOOL STOVETOP OATMEAL BUT WAY BETTER. AND IF YOU NEED A HINT MORE SWEETNESS, DON'T FORGET THE MAPLE SYRUP!

3½ CUPS	MILK	875 ML
1⅓ CUPS	LARGE-FLAKE (OLD-FASHIONED) ROLLED OATS	325 ML
3 TBSP	PACKED BROWN SUGAR	45 ML
½ TSP	GROUND CINNAMON OR PUMPKIN PIE SPICE	2 ML
1	APPLE, CORED AND DICED	1
2 TBSP	DRIED CRANBERRIES	30 ML

IN A LARGE SAUCEPAN, HEAT MILK UNTIL STEAMING. STIR IN OATS AND REDUCE HEAT TO MEDIUM-LOW HEAT; STIR IN BROWN SUGAR AND CINNAMON. COOK, STIRRING FOR ABOUT 10 MINUTES OR UNTIL ALMOST THICKENED. STIR IN APPLE AND CRANBERRIES AND COOK, STIRRING FOR ABOUT 5 MINUTES OR UNTIL THICKENED. SERVES 4.

MAKE AHEAD: MAKE THE OATMEAL THE NIGHT BEFORE AND WARM UP IN THE MICROWAVE IN THE MORNING WITH A SPLASH OF MILK. STIR AND ENJOY!

FRUIT VARIATIONS: INSTEAD OF APPLE, USE YOUR FAVORITE IN-SEASON FRUIT. TRY PEACHES, PLUMS, STRAWBERRIES, BLUEBERRIES OR PEARS.

TIP: IF YOU WANT YOUR APPLE SOFTER, SIMPLY ADD IT EARLIER AND COOK TO DESIRED TEXTURE.

TIP: FIBER UP! BE SURE TO ADD A COUPLE OF TABLESPOONS (30 ML) OF GROUND FLAX TO YOUR BOWL FOR AN EXTRA HIT OF FIBER IN THE MORNING.

TIP: DON'T FORGET YOU CAN USE FROZEN FRUIT TOO!

INSTANT POT BROWN BUTTER STEEL-CUT OATMEAL

COOKING STEEL-CUT OATS IN THE INSTANT POT IS AN EASY, HANDS-OFF WAY TO MAKE A HOT, COMFORTING BREAKFAST. THERE'S NO STANDING OVER THE STOVETOP STIRRING FREQUENTLY. ADDING A SWIRL OF OUR RASPBERRY CHIA JAM (SEE RECIPE PAGE 32) IS A FLAVORFUL WAY TO TOP THE EXTRA NUTTY OATMEAL. OTHER TASTY TOPPINGS COULD BE SLICED FRESH FRUIT, TOASTED NUTS, TOASTED COCONUT, MAPLE SYRUP OR HONEY.

3 TBSP	BUTTER	45 ML
1 1/2 CUPS	STEEL-CUT OATS	375 ML
3 1/2 CUPS	WATER	875 ML
1/4 TSP	SALT	1 ML
1 TSP	VANILLA	5 ML
	HALF-AND-HALF (10%) OR TABLE (18%) CREAM	

IN A 6-QUART INSTANT POT, SELECT SAUTÉ. ADD BUTTER AND OATS AND COOK, STIRRING OCCASIONALLY, FOR ABOUT 5 MINUTES, UNTIL OATS ARE TOASTED AND LIGHTLY GOLDEN. STIR IN WATER AND SALT. PRESS CANCEL AND LOCK LID; SET PRESSURE RELEASE VALVE TO SEALING. PRESS MANUAL PRESSURE COOK; SET TO HIGH FOR 5 MINUTES. (IT TAKES ABOUT 10 MINUTES TO COME TO PRESSURE.) WHEN COOKING FINISHES, LET THE PRESSURE RELEASE NATURALLY FOR 20 MINUTES, THEN RELEASE ANY REMAINING STEAM BY MOVING THE

PRESSURE RELEASE VALVE TO VENTING. PRESS CANCEL, OPEN LID AND STIR IN VANILLA. OATS WILL CONTINUE TO THICKEN AS IT COOLS. SERVE WARM WITH CREAM AND YOUR FAVORITE TOPPINGS. SERVES 5.

MAKE AHEAD: PREPARE AND STORE IN REFRIGERATOR FOR UP TO 4 DAYS. OR, TO FREEZE, DIVIDE COOLED OATMEAL INTO SMALLER PORTIONS IN A MUFFIN PAN OR ICE CUBE TRAY. ONCE FROZEN, STORE OATMEAL IN AN AIRTIGHT FREEZER CONTAINER. FREEZE FOR UP TO 2 MONTHS. THAW OVERNIGHT IN THE REFRIGERATOR AND REHEAT IN A POT OR MICROWAVE WITH A SPLASH OF WATER OR MILK.

SHEET-PAN BUTTERMILK CINNAMON PANCAKES

NO FLIPPING IS REQUIRED WITH THESE EASY PANCAKES BAKED IN THE OVEN. THEY'RE TENDER, FLUFFY AND GREAT FOR FEEDING A FAMILY.

2 CUPS	ALL-PURPOSE FLOUR	500 ML
3 TBSP	GRANULATED SUGAR	45 ML
2 TSP	GROUND CINNAMON	10 ML
2 TSP	BAKING POWDER	10 ML
1 TSP	BAKING SODA	5 ML
1/4 TSP	SALT	1 ML
2 CUPS	BUTTERMILK	500 ML
2	LARGE EGGS	2
3 TBSP	CANOLA OIL	45 ML
1/2 TSP	VANILLA	2 ML

PREHEAT OVEN TO 425°F (220°C). LINE AN 18- BY 13-INCH (45 BY 33 CM) RIMMED BAKING SHEET WITH PARCHMENT PAPER, LIGHTLY SPRAY WITH COOKING SPRAY; SET ASIDE.

IN A LARGE BOWL, WHISK TOGETHER FLOUR, SUGAR, CINNAMON, BAKING POWDER, BAKING SODA AND SALT. IN A MEDIUM BOWL, WHISK TOGETHER BUTTERMILK, EGGS, OIL AND VANILLA. POUR BUTTERMILK MIXTURE OVER FLOUR MIXTURE AND WHISK UNTIL JUST COMBINED BUT STILL SLIGHTLY LUMPY. POUR MIXTURE ONTO PREPARED PAN AND SPREAD BATTER TO COMPLETELY FILL BAKING SHEET.

BAKE 12 TO 15 MINUTES, UNTIL PANCAKE IS GOLDEN AND A TOOTHPICK INSERTED IN THE MIDDLE COMES OUT CLEAN. CUT PANCAKE INTO PIECES AND SERVE WITH RASPBERRY CHIA JAM (PAGE 32) OR YOUR FAVORITE FRUIT, SYRUP AND BUTTER. MAKES 12 PANCAKES.

TIP: AN 18- BY 13-INCH (45 BY 33 CM) RIMMED BAKING SHEET IS COMMONLY REFERRED TO AS A HALF-SHEET PAN.

ENTERED WHAT I ATE TODAY
INTO MY NEW FITNESS APP AND IT JUST
SENT AN AMBULANCE TO MY HOUSE.

FRENCH TOAST STICKS
WITH MAPLE ORANGE DIP

MAKE THE FRENCH TOAST AHEAD AND POP IT
IN THE TOASTER TO REHEAT. ADDING CEREAL MAKES
THE FRENCH TOAST CRUNCHY AND EXTRA TASTY.

MAPLE ORANGE DIP

1/3 CUP	ORANGE MARMALADE	75 ML
1/4 CUP	MAPLE SYRUP	60 ML
1 TSP	LEMON JUICE	5 ML
PINCH	GROUND CINNAMON	PINCH

FRENCH TOAST STICKS

1/2 CUP	MILK	125 ML
2	LARGE EGGS	2
1 TBSP	GRANULATED SUGAR	15 ML
1/2 TSP	GRATED ORANGE ZEST	2 ML
1 TSP	VANILLA	5 ML
1/2 TSP	GROUND CINNAMON	2 ML
2 CUPS	CORN FLAKES, FROSTED FLAKES OR BRAN FLAKES CEREAL, CRUSHED	500 ML
6	SLICES BRIOCHE BREAD	6
2 TBSP	BUTTER, DIVIDED	30 ML

MAPLE ORANGE DIP: IN A SMALL SAUCEPAN (OR
MICROWAVE-SAFE BOWL), HEAT MARMALADE, MAPLE SYRUP,
LEMON JUICE AND CINNAMON OVER MEDIUM-LOW HEAT
UNTIL HOT (OR MICROWAVE ON HIGH FOR 20 SECONDS).
SET ASIDE.

FRENCH TOAST STICKS: IN A SHALLOW DISH, WHISK TOGETHER MILK, EGGS, SUGAR, ZEST, VANILLA AND CINNAMON. PLACE CRUSHED CEREAL FLAKES ON A PLATE. DIP A SLICE OF BREAD IN EGG MIXTURE AND COAT BOTH SIDES WELL. DIP ONE SIDE OF THE BREAD INTO CRUSHED CEREAL.

HEAT A LARGE NONSTICK SKILLET OR GRIDDLE OVER MEDIUM-HIGH HEAT AND MELT SOME OF THE BUTTER. PLACE TWO COATED BREAD SLICES, CEREAL SIDE DOWN, AND COOK FOR ABOUT 3 MINUTES OR UNTIL GOLDEN. TURN OVER AND COOK FOR ANOTHER 2 MINUTES OR UNTIL GOLDEN. REPEAT WITH REMAINING BUTTER AND BREAD SLICES.

CUT EACH FRENCH TOAST SLICE INTO FOUR STICKS AND SERVE WITH MAPLE ORANGE DIP. SERVES 4 TO 6.

MAKE AHEAD: DO NOT SLICE FRENCH TOAST SLICES INTO STICKS. THAT WAY, YOU CAN MAKE THEM AHEAD AND POP IN THE TOASTER TO REHEAT FOR A QUICK BREAKFAST.

MAPLE CINNAMON
APPLE RICOTTA BAKE

IF YOU'RE LOOKING FOR SOMETHING A LITTLE DIFFERENT, THIS EASY, SWEET CANNOLI-INSPIRED BAKE IS CREAMY AND HAS A WONDERFUL FAMILIAR FLAVOR OF APPLES AND CINNAMON THAT IS PERFECT FOR BREAKFAST OR BRUNCH. WHO DOESN'T LOVE CANNOLI APPLE PIE FOR BREAKFAST? EMILY'S GOOD FRIEND DONNA SAID IT WAS BRILLIANT!

RICOTTA BAKE

I	TUB (500 G) RICOTTA CHEESE	I
1/3 CUP	GRANULATED SUGAR	75 ML
4	LARGE EGGS	4
2 TSP	VANILLA	10 ML

MAPLE CINNAMON APPLES

2 TBSP	BUTTER	30 ML
2	LARGE APPLES, CORED AND THINLY SLICED	2
2 TBSP	MAPLE SYRUP OR PACKED BROWN SUGAR	30 ML
2 TSP	GROUND CINNAMON	10 ML

PREHEAT OVEN TO 350°F (180°C). GREASE AN 8- OR 9-INCH (20 OR 23 CM) SQUARE BAKING DISH.

RICOTTA BAKE: IN A BOWL, WHISK TOGETHER RICOTTA CHEESE, SUGAR, EGGS AND VANILLA UNTIL SMOOTH. SPREAD INTO PREPARED DISH. BAKE FOR ABOUT 30 MINUTES OR UNTIL KNIFE INSERTED IN CENTER COMES OUT CLEAN.

MAPLE CINNAMON APPLES: MEANWHILE, IN A LARGE SKILLET, MELT BUTTER OVER MEDIUM HEAT AND COOK APPLES FOR 5 MINUTES OR UNTIL STARTING TO SOFTEN. ADD MAPLE SYRUP AND CINNAMON AND COOK, STIRRING GENTLY FOR ABOUT 3 MINUTES OR UNTIL APPLES ARE TENDER.

CUT RICOTTA BAKE INTO PIECES AND SERVE TOPPED WITH MAPLE CINNAMON APPLES. SERVES 9.

SMOKING WILL KILL YOU . . .
BACON WILL KILL YOU . . . BUT
SMOKING BACON WILL CURE IT.

BLENDER ZUCCHINI MUFFINS

WHEN YOU SHRED THE ZUCCHINI IN A FOOD PROCESSOR,
YOU CAN CONTINUE PREPARING THE MUFFINS
IN THE SAME APPLIANCE WITHOUT HAVING TO WASH
THE WORK BOWL. YAY TO FEWER DISHES TO WASH!
THE MUFFINS ARE DELICIOUS AS IS, BUT WE'VE
PROVIDED A STREUSEL-TOPPED OPTION FOR WHEN
YOU CRAVE A LITTLE EXTRA SWEETNESS.

1	MEDIUM UNPEELED ZUCCHINI	1
1/2 CUP	CANOLA OIL	125 ML
3/4 CUP	PACKED BROWN SUGAR	175 ML
2	LARGE EGGS	2
1 TSP	VANILLA	5 ML
1 CUP	ALL-PURPOSE FLOUR	250 ML
1/2 CUP	WHOLE WHEAT FLOUR	125 ML
2 TSP	GROUND CINNAMON	10 ML
1/2 TSP	BAKING SODA	2 ML
1/2 TSP	BAKING POWDER	2 ML
1/2 TSP	SALT	2 ML
1/4 TSP	GROUND NUTMEG	1 ML

PREHEAT OVEN TO 375°F (190°C). GREASE A 12-CUP
MUFFIN PAN OR LINE IT WITH PAPER LINERS. IN A FOOD
PROCESSOR FITTED WITH A GRATER ATTACHMENT,
GRATE ZUCCHINI. MEASURE OUT 1 3/4 CUPS (425 ML)
GRATED ZUCCHINI AND TRANSFER TO A SMALL BOWL.
(ANY LEFTOVER ZUCCHINI CAN BE USED IN A SALAD,
ADDED TO SOUP OR SAUTÉED.) IN THE SAME FOOD
PROCESSOR BOWL, WITHOUT WASHING IT AND USING

THE MULTI-PURPOSE BLADE, ADD OIL, BROWN SUGAR, EGGS AND VANILLA; PROCESS 5 SECONDS. REMOVE LID AND ADD FLOURS, CINNAMON, BAKING SODA, BAKING POWDER, SALT AND NUTMEG. PULSE 10 TIMES, OR UNTIL INGREDIENTS ARE MOSTLY BLENDED. STOP PROCESSOR, SCRAPE DOWN THE INSIDE OF THE BOWL AND ADD ZUCCHINI; PULSE 5 TO 6 TIMES, UNTIL JUST BLENDED. DO NOT OVERMIX.

DIVIDE THE BATTER INTO PREPARED MUFFIN PAN. BAKE 20 TO 25 MINUTES, OR UNTIL AN INSERTED TOOTHPICK COMES OUT CLEAN. COOL IN PAN FOR 5 MINUTES, THEN TRANSFER MUFFINS ONTO A RACK TO FINISH COOLING. SERVES 12.

TIP: MUFFINS ARE BEST FRESH, BUT WILL KEEP IN AN AIRTIGHT CONTAINER AT ROOM TEMPERATURE FOR 2 DAYS. MUFFINS CAN ALSO BE FROZEN IN AN AIRTIGHT CONTAINER FOR UP TO 2 MONTHS.

STREUSEL-TOPPED VARIATION

1/4 CUP	ALL-PURPOSE FLOUR	60 ML
3 TBSP	PACKED BROWN SUGAR	45 ML
1/4 TSP	GROUND CINNAMON	1 ML
2 TBSP	BUTTER, MELTED	30 ML

IN A SMALL BOWL, COMBINE FLOUR, BROWN SUGAR, CINNAMON AND BUTTER UNTIL CRUMBLY MIXTURE FORMS. SPRINKLE ON TOP OF MUFFINS JUST BEFORE BAKING.

EGG IN A HOLE

THIS CLASSIC BREAKFAST CAN BE CHANGED UP IN SO MANY WAYS, EVERY MORNING CAN BE A SURPRISE! AND IT'S READY TO EAT IN UNDER 15 MINUTES.

1	SLICE BREAD	1
2 TSP	CANOLA OIL	10 ML
1	LARGE EGG	1
PINCH	EACH SALT AND BLACK PEPPER	PINCH
2 TBSP	DICED RED BELL PEPPER OR MUSHROOMS	30 ML
2 TBSP	SHREDDED CHEESE (OPTIONAL)	30 ML

USING A 3-INCH (7.5 CM) COOKIE CUTTER, CUT A HOLE IN THE CENTER OF THE BREAD SLICE.

IN A SMALL NONSTICK SKILLET, HEAT OIL OVER MEDIUM HEAT.

IN A SMALL BOWL, BEAT EGG WITH SALT AND PEPPER. STIR IN RED PEPPER. POUR INTO HOLE IN BREAD AND LET COOK FOR 2 MINUTES. SPRINKLE WITH CHEESE, IF USING, AND PLACE BREAD CIRCLE INTO CENTER OF EGG MIXTURE. USING A SPATULA, FLIP BREAD AND EGG OVER AND COOK FOR ABOUT 2 MINUTES OR UNTIL EGG IS SET AND BREAD IS GOLDEN. SERVES 1.

VARIATIONS: YOU CAN USE A ROUND SLICE OF RED PEPPER OR LARGE, ROUND SLICE OF ONION INSTEAD OF THE BREAD TO ENJOY YOUR EGG IN.

TIP: NO COOKIE CUTTER? NO PROBLEM. SIMPLY USE A KNIFE TO CUT THE HOLE.

*THOSE LITTLE RAMEKINS OR CUSTARD CUPS
WE HAVE IN OUR CUPBOARDS NEED TO BE PUT TO
GOOD USE — SO BREAKFAST IS THE ANSWER!*

1/4 CUP	BRICK-STYLE CREAM CHEESE, CUT INTO 4 CUBES	60 ML
4	LARGE EGGS	4
1/4 CUP	HEAVY OR WHIPPING (35%) CREAM	60 ML
1 TBSP	CHOPPED FRESH PARSLEY OR BASIL	15 ML
1/4 TSP	EACH SALT AND BLACK PEPPER	1 ML
1/4 CUP	SHREDDED CHEDDAR CHEESE (OPTIONAL)	60 ML

PREHEAT OVEN TO 400°F (200°C). PLACE FOUR 1/2-CUP (125 ML) RAMEKINS ON A SMALL BAKING SHEET. SPRAY EACH WITH COOKING SPRAY. ADD A CUBE OF CREAM CHEESE TO EACH RAMEKIN, THEN CRACK 1 EGG INTO EACH.

IN A SMALL BOWL, WHISK TOGETHER CREAM, PARSLEY, SALT AND PEPPER. POUR OVER TOP OF EACH EGG. SPRINKLE WITH CHEESE, IF USING.

BAKE FOR ABOUT 10 MINUTES OR UNTIL EGG IS SET, CHEESE IS MELTED AND EDGES ARE BUBBLY. SERVES 4.

TIP: BE SURE TO STIR UP THE RAMEKIN BEFORE ENJOYING FOR A TASTE OF EVERYTHING IN ONE BITE.

MAKE AHEAD: BAKE RAMEKIN EGGS AHEAD AND KEEP COVERED IN THE REFRIGERATOR FOR UP TO 3 DAYS. WARM THE RAMEKIN EGG IN MICROWAVE AND SLIP IT ON A TOASTED ENGLISH MUFFIN FOR A TASTY MORNING SANDWICH!

YOU CAN MAKE EGGS BENEDICT WITHOUT THE HOLLANDAISE SAUCE AND STILL HAVE A WINNING BREAKFAST EXPERIENCE. EMILY MAKES THESE AT HOME AND FOUR OUT OF FIVE PEOPLE IN HER HOUSE AGREE THAT THEY ARE DELISH!

2	ENGLISH MUFFINS, SPLIT	2
4	SLICES PROCESSED CHEESE	4
4	SLICES BACON, COOKED	4
2 TSP	WHITE VINEGAR	10 ML
4	LARGE EGGS	4
1/4 CUP	SHREDDED MOZZARELLA-CHEDDAR CHEESE BLEND	60 ML
	SALT AND BLACK PEPPER	

TOAST THE ENGLISH MUFFINS AND PLACE ON A BAKING SHEET, CUT SIDE UP. TOP EACH WITH CHEESE AND BACON; SET ASIDE. PREHEAT OVEN TO 400°F (200°C).

POUR ENOUGH WATER INTO A LARGE, DEEP SKILLET TO COME 2 INCHES (5 CM) UP THE SIDE. BRING TO A BOIL. REDUCE HEAT TO A SIMMER AND ADD VINEGAR. BREAK 1 EGG INTO A SMALL BOWL AND GENTLY SLIP EGG INTO THE WATER. REPEAT FOR EACH EGG. COOK FOR 3 TO 5 MINUTES OR UNTIL DESIRED DONENESS.

USING A SLOTTED SPOON, REMOVE EGGS TO A PLATE LINED WITH A PAPER TOWEL. PLACE 1 EGG ON EACH ENGLISH MUFFIN AND SPRINKLE WITH CHEESE.

BAKE FOR ABOUT 5 MINUTES OR UNTIL CHEESE IS MELTED.
SEASON TO TASTE WITH SALT AND PEPPER IF DESIRED.
SERVES 2 TO 4.

VARIATION: SUBSTITUTE SMOKED HAM, COOKED PEAMEAL
BACON OR SMOKED SALMON FOR THE SLICED BACON.

MAKE AHEAD: IF COOKING FOR A LARGE CROWD, POACH THE
EGGS AHEAD OF TIME. POACH THEM FOR 3 MINUTES, THEN
USE A SLOTTED SPOON TO TRANSFER THEM TO A BOWL
OF ICE WATER. ONCE FIRM, REFRIGERATE POACHED EGGS
IN WATER FOR UP TO 1 DAY. HEAT A POT OF WATER TO
STEAMING, SLIP THE COLD EGGS IN AND HEAT THROUGH
TO SERVE WARM.

WHAT IS A CHICKEN RACING DRIVER'S
FAVORITE PART OF THE CAR?
THE EGGS-CELERATOR.

BLUEBERRY PECAN OAT SCONES

PERFECT WITH A CUP OF TEA OR COFFEE,
THESE FLAKY, TENDER AND CRISP SCONES
ARE SATISFYING ANY TIME OF THE DAY.

1½ CUPS	ALL-PURPOSE FLOUR	375 ML
½ CUP	QUICK-COOKING ROLLED OATS	125 ML
¼ CUP	PACKED BROWN SUGAR	60 ML
1 TBSP	BAKING POWDER	15 ML
½ TSP	BAKING SODA	2 ML
½ TSP	SALT	2 ML
½ CUP	COLD BUTTER, CUBED	125 ML
1 CUP	FRESH BLUEBERRIES	250 ML
⅓ CUP	CHOPPED TOASTED PECANS	75 ML
¾ CUP	BUTTERMILK	175 ML

PREHEAT OVEN TO 425°F (220°C); SET ASIDE A LIGHTLY
GREASED OR PARCHMENT PAPER LINED BAKING SHEET. IN
A LARGE BOWL, COMBINE FLOUR, OATS, BROWN SUGAR,
BAKING POWDER, BAKING SODA AND SALT. ADD BUTTER;
USING A PASTRY BLENDER OR TWO FORKS, CUT IN BUTTER
UNTIL MIXTURE IS CRUMBLY. GENTLY STIR IN BLUEBERRIES
AND PECANS. ADD BUTTERMILK AND GENTLY COMBINE
TO MAKE A RAGGED DOUGH. ON A LIGHTLY FLOURED
SURFACE, PAT DOUGH INTO A 10- BY 5-INCH (25 BY 12.5 CM)
RECTANGLE, ABOUT ½ INCH (1 CM) THICK; DIVIDE INTO
10 PIECES. TRANSFER TO PREPARED BAKING SHEET.

MAKE AHEAD: DOUGH CAN BE COVERED AND REFRIGERATED OVERNIGHT. THE NEXT MORNING WHEN YOU ARE READY TO BAKE, PLACE SCONES ON PREPARED BAKING SHEET WHILE THE OVEN IS PREHEATING. BAKE AS DIRECTED.

BAKE 20 TO 25 MINUTES, UNTIL GOLDEN. TRANSFER TO A RACK TO COOL. SERVES 10.

TIP: STORE IN AN AIRTIGHT CONTAINER FOR UP TO 24 HOURS OR FREEZE IN AN AIRTIGHT FREEZER-SAFE CONTAINER FOR UP TO 2 WEEKS.

TOASTED OAT GRANOLA CEREAL SQUARES

EACH TIME YOU MAKE THESE TASTY SQUARES YOU CAN CHANGE THEM UP WITH WHATEVER CEREAL YOU HAVE ON HAND. TOASTING THE OATS ADDS BIG FLAVOR TO THIS SIMPLE NO-BAKE DISH.

1½ CUPS	LARGE-FLAKE (OLD-FASHIONED) ROLLED OATS	375 ML
½ CUP	CHOPPED ALMONDS (OPTIONAL)	125 ML
1 CUP	CORN FLAKES, BRAN FLAKES OR FROSTED FLAKES CEREAL	250 ML
1 CUP	MEDJOOL DATES, PITTED (ABOUT 10 DATES)	250 ML
¼ CUP	LIQUID HONEY	60 ML
¼ CUP	ALMOND OR PEANUT BUTTER OR NUT BUTTER ALTERNATIVE	60 ML

GREASE AN 8- OR 9-INCH (20 OR 23 CM) SQUARE BAKING PAN AND SET ASIDE. IN A LARGE NONSTICK SKILLET, TOAST OATS AND ALMONDS (IF USING) OVER MEDIUM HEAT, STIRRING OFTEN FOR ABOUT 5 MINUTES OR UNTIL LIGHT GOLDEN AND FRAGRANT. POUR INTO A LARGE BOWL AND LET COOL SLIGHTLY; STIR IN CORN FLAKES.

IN THE BOWL OF A FOOD PROCESSOR, PULSE DATES UNTIL FINELY CHOPPED. (THEY MAY BALL UP A BIT.)

IN A SMALL SAUCEPAN, HEAT TOGETHER HONEY AND PEANUT BUTTER OVER MEDIUM-LOW HEAT UNTIL MELTED AND SMOOTH. ADD DATES AND STIR TO COMBINE. POUR INTO OAT MIXTURE AND STIR TOGETHER UNTIL

DATES ARE DISTRIBUTED EVENLY THROUGHOUT AND OATS ARE WELL COATED. (IF YOU'RE ABLE TO, SPRAY YOUR HANDS WITH COOKING SPRAY AND MIX EVERYTHING TOGETHER WITH YOUR HANDS.)

PLACE MIXTURE IN PREPARED PAN AND PRESS TO FLATTEN EVENLY. COVER AND REFRIGERATE FOR AT LEAST 1 HOUR OR UNTIL FIRM. CUT INTO SQUARES, WRAP INDIVIDUALLY WITH PLASTIC WRAP AND STORE IN REFRIGERATOR FOR UP TO 1 WEEK. MAKES 12 SQUARES.

CHOCOLATE CHIP OR DRIED FRUIT VARIATION: SPRINKLE 2 TBSP (30 ML) MINI CHOCOLATE CHIPS OR CHOPPED DRIED CRANBERRIES OR APRICOTS ON TOP OF GRANOLA MIXTURE AND PRESS INTO TOP BEFORE REFRIGERATING.

COCONUT VARIATION: SPRINKLE 2 TBSP (30 ML) UNSWEETENED SHREDDED COCONUT ON TOP OF GRANOLA MIXTURE AND PRESS INTO TOP BEFORE REFRIGERATING.

GLUTEN-FREE OPTION: USE GLUTEN-FREE OATS AND BREAKFAST CEREAL IN THE RECIPE.

OATMEAL CHOCO-CRANBERRY MORNING COOKIES

KIDS CAN HAVE VARIOUS ALLERGIES, SO SOMETIMES MAKING SNACKS CAN BE TRICKY. IN THESE COOKIES, NO EGG OR FLOUR IS USED. THESE COOKIES HAVE A SOFT TEXTURE WITH AN ADDICTIVE TASTE.

2	VERY RIPE BANANAS	2
1/2 TSP	VANILLA	2 ML
I CUP	LARGE-FLAKE (OLD-FASHIONED) ROLLED OATS	250 ML
2 TBSP	GROUND FLAX OR CHIA SEED (OPTIONAL)	30 ML
1/4 TSP	GROUND CINNAMON	I ML
3 TBSP	MINI CHOCOLATE CHIPS	45 ML
3 TBSP	DRIED CRANBERRIES	45 ML

PREHEAT OVEN TO 350°F (180°C). LINE A BAKING SHEET WITH PARCHMENT PAPER; SET ASIDE. IN A BOWL, MASH BANANAS UNTIL SMOOTH. STIR IN VANILLA.

IN ANOTHER BOWL, STIR TOGETHER OATS, FLAX (IF USING) AND CINNAMON. STIR INTO BANANA MIXTURE UNTIL WELL COMBINED. STIR IN CHOCOLATE CHIPS AND CRANBERRIES.

SCOOP DOUGH INTO 12 MOUNDS ONTO PREPARED BAKING SHEET. FLATTEN EACH SLIGHTLY AND BAKE IN OVEN FOR ABOUT 12 MINUTES OR UNTIL COOKIES ARE FIRM TO THE TOUCH. LET COOL BEFORE REMOVING FROM BAKING SHEET. MAKES 12 COOKIES.

TIP: YOU CAN FIND GLUTEN-FREE OATS AS WELL AS ALLERGEN-FREE CHOCOLATE AND DRIED FRUIT IN HEALTH FOOD STORES AND IN WELL-STOCKED SUPERMARKETS.

MAKE AHEAD: PLACE IN AN AIRTIGHT CONTAINER AND KEEP AT ROOM TEMPERATURE FOR UP TO 3 DAYS OR REFRIGERATED FOR UP TO 1 WEEK.

RASPBERRY CHIA JAM

TASTY AND TART, THIS QUICK-TO-PREPARE JAM CAN
BE MADE WITHOUT CANNING EQUIPMENT.

3 CUPS	RASPBERRIES	750 ML
1 TBSP	LEMON JUICE	15 ML
1 TBSP	GRANULATED SUGAR	15 ML
PINCH	SALT	PINCH
2 TBSP	CHIA SEEDS	30 ML

IN A MEDIUM SAUCEPAN, COMBINE RASPBERRIES, LEMON
JUICE, SUGAR AND SALT. COOK OVER MEDIUM-LOW HEAT,
STIRRING OCCASIONALLY FOR 5 MINUTES. SLIGHTLY
MASH FRUIT WITH A FORK OR POTATO MASHER, LEAVING
A FEW CHUNKS. STIR IN CHIA; COOK AN ADDITIONAL
3 MINUTES. REMOVE FROM HEAT AND ALLOW TO COOL
15 MINUTES; MIXTURE WILL CONTINUE TO THICKEN. STIR
AND TRANSFER TO AN AIRTIGHT CONTAINER. MAKES
ABOUT 1 1/4 CUPS (300 ML).

TIP: FROZEN RASPBERRIES CAN BE USED. MEASURE BERRIES
WHILE THEY ARE STILL FROZEN. THAW IN SAUCEPAN
BEFORE PROCEEDING WITH RECIPE.

TIP: FREEZE JAM IN AN ICE CUBE TRAY FOR PORTIONING.
ONCE SOLID, POP OUT OF THE MOLD AND TRANSFER TO
A FREEZER-SAFE CONTAINER.

MAKE AHEAD: COVER AND STORE IN THE REFRIGERATOR
FOR UP TO 2 WEEKS OR FREEZE IN A FREEZER-SAFE
CONTAINER FOR UP TO 2 MONTHS.

APPETIZERS

CARAMELIZED ONION AND BLUE CHEESE TARTLETS

THESE TARTS COMBINE THE RICH DECADENCE OF BLUE CHEESE WITH SWEET, LUSCIOUS ONIONS IN A TENDER PASTRY BITE. THEY ARE DEFINITELY ONE APPETIZER THAT WILL BE THE HIT OF ANY COCKTAIL PARTY.

PASTRY

2 CUPS	ALL-PURPOSE FLOUR	500 ML
2 TBSP	GRANULATED SUGAR	30 ML
1/4 TSP	SALT	I ML
1/2 CUP	COLD BUTTER, CUBED	125 ML
2	LARGE EGG YOLKS	2
3 TBSP	WATER (APPROX.)	45 ML

FILLING

I TBSP	CANOLA OIL	15 ML
I	LARGE ONION, THINLY SLICED	I
1/4 CUP	WATER OR DRY WHITE WINE	60 ML
2 OZ	GORGONZOLA OR OTHER BLUE CHEESE (SEE TIP)	60 G
3/4 CUP	HEAVY OR WHIPPING (35%) CREAM (APPROX.)	175 ML

PASTRY: IN A FOOD PROCESSOR, PULSE TOGETHER FLOUR, SUGAR AND SALT. ADD BUTTER; PULSE TO BREAK UP BUTTER. ADD EGG YOLKS AND WATER I TBSP (15 ML) AT A TIME; PULSE UNTIL DOUGH STARTS TO CLUMP. DUMP MIXTURE ONTO COUNTER AND KNEAD GENTLY TO BRING DOUGH TOGETHER. DIVIDE DOUGH IN HALF AND DIVIDE EACH HALF INTO 12 SMALL EQUAL PIECES.

PLACE DOUGH PIECES INTO 24-CUP MINI MUFFIN PAN. USING A TART TAMPER OR YOUR FINGERS, PRESS EVENLY

INTO BOTTOMS AND UP SIDES OF PAN. REFRIGERATE FOR ABOUT 30 MINUTES OR UNTIL FIRM.

FILLING: MEANWHILE, IN A LARGE SKILLET, HEAT OIL OVER MEDIUM HEAT; COOK ONIONS, STIRRING FOR ABOUT 10 MINUTES OR UNTIL STARTING TO BECOME GOLDEN. ADD WATER; REDUCE HEAT AND COVER AND COOK FOR ABOUT 10 MINUTES OR UNTIL BROWN AND SOFT. LET COOL. PREHEAT OVEN TO 425°F (220°C).

DIVIDE ONIONS AND BLUE CHEESE AMONG TART SHELLS. POUR CREAM INTO EACH TART TO COVER. BAKE FOR ABOUT 15 MINUTES OR UNTIL GOLDEN. LET COOL COMPLETELY IN PAN ON RACK. MAKES 24 TARTS.

TIP: IF YOU CAN'T FIND GORGONZOLA, SUBSTITUTE YOUR FAVORITE BLUE CHEESE SUCH AS STILTON OR A CREAMY DANISH BLUE.

MAKE AHEAD: COVER AND REFRIGERATE TARTS FOR UP TO 3 DAYS. REHEAT IN 350°F (180°C) OVEN FOR ABOUT 5 MINUTES OR UNTIL PASTRY IS WARM.

TIP: IF YOU DON'T WANT TO MAKE YOUR OWN PASTRY, USE 24 FROZEN MINI TART SHELLS FROM THE FREEZER SECTION OF YOUR GROCER. FOR LARGER TARTS, USE 12 TART SHELLS INSTEAD.

TIP: TO SERVE ON GREENS, SIMPLY TOSS GREENS WITH A LIGHT VINAIGRETTE AND TOP WITH TART. IF DESIRED, SPRINKLE WITH ALMONDS AND MORE GORGONZOLA TO SERVE.

PEPPER JELLY TARTS

THIS PERFECT ONE-BITE APPETIZER IS CHEESY,
SWEET AND A LITTLE SPICY. YOU MIGHT WANT
TO MAKE A DOUBLE BATCH BECAUSE THEY'LL
GET DEVOURED IN A FLASH.

1 CUP	ALL-PURPOSE FLOUR	250 ML
2 TBSP	CORNSTARCH	30 ML
1 TSP	SMOKED PAPRIKA	5 ML
1/4 CUP	FINELY CHOPPED WALNUTS	60 ML
1/2 CUP	BUTTER, SOFTENED	125 ML
2 CUPS	SHREDDED SHARP (OLD) CHEDDAR CHEESE (ABOUT 8 OZ/250 G)	500 ML
1/4 CUP	HOT PEPPER JELLY	60 ML

PREHEAT OVEN TO 375°F (190°C). LIGHTLY GREASE A 24-CUP
MINI MUFFIN PAN (OR TWO 12-CUP MINI MUFFIN PANS). IN
A MEDIUM BOWL, WHISK TOGETHER FLOUR, CORNSTARCH,
PAPRIKA AND WALNUTS; SET ASIDE. IN A LARGE BOWL,
USING AN ELECTRIC MIXER, BEAT BUTTER AND CHEESE
UNTIL BLENDED. STIR IN FLOUR MIXTURE UNTIL COMBINED;
DOUGH WILL BE VERY CRUMBLY. USE YOUR HANDS TO
PRESS THE DOUGH TOGETHER.

USING A SMALL ICE-CREAM SCOOP OR TABLESPOON
(15 ML), SCOOP UP DOUGH, ROLL INTO BALLS AND PRESS
INTO PREPARED MUFFIN PAN. PRESS YOUR THUMB IN THE
CENTER OF EACH BALL AND THEN BAKE 15 TO 20 MINUTES
UNTIL LIGHTLY GOLDEN.

REMOVE FROM OVEN AND, USING THE TIP OF A WOODEN SPOON HANDLE, GENTLY PRESS PUFFED CENTERS DOWN. LET COOL IN PAN FOR 15 MINUTES, THEN REMOVE FROM PAN. SPOON A LITTLE PEPPER JELLY INTO EACH INDENT. MAKES 24 TARTS.

MAKE AHEAD: UNFILLED TARTS CAN BE PREPARED 3 DAYS IN ADVANCE AND STORED IN AN AIRTIGHT CONTAINER. TARTS CAN ALSO BE FROZEN FOR UP TO 1 MONTH. FILL WITH JELLY WHEN READY TO SERVE.

TIP: HOT PEPPER JELLY IS AVAILABLE IN DIFFERENT COLORS AND FLAVORS. EXPERIMENT AND FILL TARTS WITH A VARIETY OF PEPPER JELLIES.

THE DINNER I WAS COOKING FOR MY FAMILY WAS GOING TO BE A SURPRISE BUT THE FIRETRUCKS RUINED IT.

THIS IS A DELICIOUS AND CREAMY NACHO-FLAVORED DIP THAT ADULTS AND KIDS WILL LOVE. IT'S AN EASY WAY TO START THE EVENING WITH FRIENDS OR ENJOY WHILE WATCHING THE GAME. AND, AS EMILY'S FRIEND HEATHER SAYS, "OF COURSE WE ARE SERVING IT WITH DRINKS!"

8 OZ	BRICK-STYLE CREAM CHEESE, SOFTENED	250 G
1 CUP	MEDIUM SALSA	250 ML
1 1/2 CUPS	SHREDDED SHARP (OLD) CHEDDAR CHEESE, DIVIDED	375 ML
1/4 CUP	CHOPPED PICKLED JALAPEÑO PEPPERS	60 ML
1	BAG (275 G) TORTILLA CHIPS	1

PREHEAT OVEN TO 350°F (180°C). SET ASIDE A 9-INCH (23 CM) PIE PLATE.

IN A LARGE BOWL, BEAT TOGETHER CREAM CHEESE, SALSA AND 1 CUP (250 ML) OF THE CHEDDAR CHEESE UNTIL COMBINED. STIR IN JALAPEÑO PEPPERS AND SPREAD INTO PIE PLATE. SPRINKLE WITH REMAINING CHEDDAR CHEESE. BAKE FOR ABOUT 20 MINUTES OR UNTIL CHEESE IS MELTED AND BUBBLY AROUND EDGES. SERVE WITH CHIPS. SERVES 6 TO 8.

EXTRA HOT: USE HOT SALSA AND DOUBLE UP ON THE JALAPEÑOS FOR SOME REAL SPICE.

TIPS: LOOK FOR LIME-FLAVORED TORTILLA CHIPS FOR SOME WONDERFUL FLAVOR TO GO WITH THE DIP. NOT A FAN OF TORTILLA CHIPS? USE THICK-CUT KETTLE OR WAVY CHIPS FOR DIPPING.

POTATO-CHIP BACON CHEDDAR BOWLS

THIS FUN IDEA GIVES EVERYONE THEIR OWN BOWL TO ENJOY! WHETHER YOU CUT IT WITH A FORK AND KNIFE OR PULL IT APART TO EAT IT, THE TASTE IS WHAT WILL KEEP YOU COMING BACK FOR MORE.

8 OZ	BRICK-STYLE CREAM CHEESE, SOFTENED	250 G
1½ CUPS	SHREDDED SHARP (OLD) CHEDDAR CHEESE, DIVIDED	375 ML
½ CUP	HEAVY OR WHIPPING (35%) CREAM	125 ML
½ CUP	CHOPPED COOKED BACON	125 ML
2	GREEN ONIONS, CHOPPED AND DIVIDED	2
2 CUPS	POTATO CHIPS	500 ML
6	SOFT KAISER BUNS	6

PREHEAT OVEN TO 350°F (180°C). SET ASIDE A BAKING SHEET. IN A LARGE BOWL, BEAT TOGETHER CREAM CHEESE, 1 CUP (250 ML) OF THE CHEESE, CREAM, BACON AND HALF OF THE GREEN ONIONS UNTIL COMBINED; SET ASIDE. CRUSH POTATO CHIPS AND STIR INTO MIXTURE.

CUT A LARGE, DEEP HOLE INTO THE KAISER BUNS, RESERVING THE BREAD YOU CUT OUT. SPOON THE CREAM CHEESE MIXTURE INTO EACH BUN. SPRINKLE TOPS WITH REMAINING CHEESE. PLACE FILLED BUNS ON BAKING SHEET AND BAKE FOR ABOUT 20 MINUTES OR UNTIL BUNS ARE TOASTED AND CHEESE IS WARMED THROUGH. SPRINKLE WITH REMAINING GREEN ONION AND SERVE WITH BUN CUT-OUTS AND MORE CHIPS, IF DESIRED. SERVES 4.

CROSTINI

THESE ADDICTIVE LITTLE CRUNCHY BITES ARE WONDERFUL ON THEIR OWN, BUT PUT TOPPINGS ON THEM AND, WELL, YOU MAY WANT TO DOUBLE THE RECIPE!

1	BAGUETTE, SLICED	1
1/4 CUP	EXTRA VIRGIN OLIVE OIL	60 ML
1/2 TSP	EACH SALT AND BLACK PEPPER	2 ML

PREHEAT OVEN TO 400°F (200°C). BRUSH BAGUETTE SLICES WITH OIL. PLACE ON LARGE BAKING SHEET IN A SINGLE LAYER. TOAST IN OVEN FOR ABOUT 8 MINUTES OR UNTIL THEY ARE LIGHT GOLDEN AND STILL A BIT SOFT IN THE CENTER. SPRINKLE WITH SALT AND PEPPER. MAKES ABOUT 12 PIECES.

TIP: YOU CAN ALSO GRILL THE BAGUETTE SLICES FOR A SMOKY FLAVOR.

MAKE-AHEAD: YOU CAN MAKE THE CROSTINI UP TO 1 DAY AHEAD. RECRISP IN 350°F (180°C) OVEN FOR A FEW MINUTES IF DESIRED BEFORE USING.

GARLIC-RUBBED VARIATION: CUT 1 LARGE GARLIC CLOVE LENGTHWISE AND RUB GARLIC OVER BAGUETTE SLICES WHILE THEY ARE STILL WARM.

ROASTED TOMATOES AND FETA CROSTINI

ROASTED TOMATOES AND FETA HAVE ALWAYS BEEN
A TASTY COMBINATION. BEST OF BRIDGE FANS
LOVE THIS COMBO OVER AND OVER AGAIN.

3 CUPS	GRAPE TOMATOES	750 ML
6	GARLIC CLOVES, PEELED	6
2 TBSP	CHOPPED FRESH BASIL	30 ML
I TSP	CHOPPED FRESH ROSEMARY	5 ML
1/4 TSP	EACH SALT AND BLACK PEPPER	I ML
3 TBSP	EXTRA VIRGIN OLIVE OIL	45 ML
I CUP	DICED FETA CHEESE	250 ML
I	BATCH GARLIC-RUBBED CROSTINI (SEE RECIPE PAGE 40)	I
	BALSAMIC GLAZE (OPTIONAL)	

PREHEAT OVEN TO 400°F (200°C). LINE BAKING SHEET
WITH PARCHMENT PAPER. IN A BOWL, COMBINE
TOMATOES, GARLIC, BASIL, ROSEMARY, SALT, PEPPER
AND OIL. SPREAD ONTO PREPARED PAN AND ROAST FOR
15 MINUTES. STIR IN FETA CHEESE AND RETURN TO
OVEN FOR ABOUT 10 MINUTES OR UNTIL FETA IS GOLDEN
BROWN AND TOMATOES ARE GOLDEN AND STARTING TO
BURST. LET COOL SLIGHTLY AND SPOON ONTO CROSTINI
TO ENJOY. DRIZZLE WITH BALSAMIC GLAZE IF DESIRED.
MAKES ABOUT 24 PIECES.

RICOTTA AND WINE
HONEY FIG CROSTINI

DRIED FIGS HAVE A WONDERFUL SWEET TASTE THAT
CAN MAKE RICOTTA CHEESE SING. USE YOUR FAVORITE
RED WINE TO COOK THE FIGS IN, SO YOU CAN ENJOY
A SIP OR TWO WHILE THEY SIMMER AWAY.

I	PACKAGE (7 OZ/200 G) DRIED FIGS	I
3/4 CUP	DRY RED WINE	175 ML
I TBSP	LIQUID HONEY	15 ML
I	CINNAMON STICK	I
I	BATCH CROSTINI (SEE PAGE 40)	I
3/4 CUP	RICOTTA CHEESE	175 ML
	SALT	

REMOVE TOUGH STEM END OF FIG AND CUT EACH FIG IN
HALF LENGTHWISE.

IN A SMALL SAUCEPAN, BRING FIGS, WINE, HONEY AND
CINNAMON STICK TO BOIL. REDUCE HEAT TO A GENTLE
SIMMER; COVER AND COOK FOR ABOUT 10 MINUTES OR
UNTIL FIGS ARE VERY SOFT AND PLUMP. SET ASIDE.

SPREAD CROSTINI WITH RICOTTA CHEESE. SPRINKLE
RICOTTA LIGHTLY WITH SALT, TO TASTE. TOP EACH
WITH 2 FIG HALVES AND DRIZZLE WITH SOME OF THE
REMAINING SYRUP. MAKES ABOUT 16 PIECES.

EDAMAME LEMON HUMMUS

PICK UP A FEW BAGS OF EDAMAME AND KEEP THEM
IN THE FREEZER FOR SNACKS, SIDE DISH OPTIONS
AND THIS REFRESHING HUMMUS! IT IS PERFECT
TO SERVE WITH POTATO OR TORTILLA CHIPS.

1 CUP	FROZEN SHELLED EDAMAME (GREEN SOYBEANS)	250 ML
1 CUP	CANNED CHICKPEAS, RINSED AND DRAINED	250 ML
1/4 CUP	CHOPPED FRESH BASIL	60 ML
1/4 CUP	CHOPPED FRESH MINT	60 ML
1 TSP	GRATED LEMON ZEST	5 ML
3 TBSP	LEMON JUICE	45 ML
1/4 CUP	WATER OR VEGETABLE BROTH	60 ML
3 TBSP	CANOLA OIL	45 ML
	SALT AND BLACK PEPPER	

IN A SAUCEPAN OF BOILING WATER, COOK EDAMAME FOR
ABOUT 5 MINUTES OR UNTIL TENDER AND PLUMP. DRAIN
WELL AND LET COOL SLIGHTLY.

PLACE IN FOOD PROCESSOR WITH CHICKPEAS, BASIL,
MINT, LEMON ZEST AND JUICE. PULSE A FEW TIMES UNTIL
COARSE. ADD WATER AND OIL AND PUREÉ UNTIL SMOOTH.
STIR IN SALT AND PEPPER TO TASTE. MAKES ABOUT
2 CUPS (500 ML).

TIP: TRY THIS HUMMUS AS A SPREAD ON YOUR NEXT
SANDWICH OR WRAP FOR ADDED FLAVOR AND PROTEIN. OR
SERVE IT UP WITH YOUR FAVORITE VEGGIES LIKE SLICED
CUCUMBER OR CARROTS.

PAM'S HERB AND SHALLOT-MARINATED SHRIMP

THERE HAVE BEEN MANY GATHERINGS WHEN
EMILY'S FRIEND PAM MAKES THESE DELICIOUS
SHRIMP, AND NO MATTER WHO'S THERE, SOMEONE
IS BOUND TO ASK FOR THE RECIPE. SO NOW, NO
ONE HAS TO ASK HER ANYMORE — IT'S RIGHT HERE!
PLEASE DO MAKE IT; IF YOU'RE A SHRIMP LOVER,
YOU WILL NOT BE DISAPPOINTED.

3 LB	LARGE RAW SHRIMP, THAWED, SHELLED AND DEVEINED	1.5 KG
1/3 CUP	EXTRA VIRGIN OLIVE OIL	75 ML
1/4 CUP	CHOPPED FRESH PARSLEY	60 ML
1/4 CUP	FINELY CHOPPED SHALLOTS	60 ML
1/4 CUP	CIDER VINEGAR	60 ML
1/4 CUP	WHITE WINE VINEGAR	60 ML
1/4 CUP	DIJON MUSTARD	60 ML
2 TSP	HOT PEPPER FLAKES	10 ML
	SALT AND BLACK PEPPER	

IN A POT OF SIMMERING WATER, COOK SHRIMP FOR
ABOUT 4 MINUTES OR UNTIL JUST PINK. DRAIN WELL
AND TRANSFER TO A LARGE BOWL.

IN A SMALL BOWL, WHISK TOGETHER OIL, PARSLEY,
SHALLOTS, CIDER VINEGAR AND WHITE WINE VINEGAR,
MUSTARD AND HOT PEPPER FLAKES. POUR OVER SHRIMP
AND STIR TO COAT WELL. COVER AND REFRIGERATE FOR

AT LEAST 4 HOURS (BUT OVERNIGHT IS EVEN BETTER) OR
UNTIL COLD. SEASON TO TASTE WITH SALT AND PEPPER
IF DESIRED.

BE SURE TO SERVE IT WITH ALL THE DELICIOUS JUICES,
AS THEY ARE TASTY SOPPED UP WITH BREAD! SERVES 6
TO 8.

TIP: SERVE THE SHRIMP AS A SALAD AND USE THE
MARINADE AS THE DRESSING FOR SALAD GREENS;
YOU WILL LOVE IT.

TURNING VEGAN IS A BIG MISSED STEAK.

SHAN'S SUSHI BAKE

WHEN EMILY FIRST ENJOYED THIS, SHE COULDN'T STOP AT JUST ONE BITE! NO ONE CAN IF THEY LOVE SUSHI. SHAN MAKES THEM TWO AT A TIME TO MAKE SURE THERE IS ENOUGH FOR EVERYONE AROUND OR TO SHARE WITH FRIENDS.

1½ CUPS	WATER	375 ML
1 CUP	SUSHI (CALROSE) RICE	250 ML
½ TSP	SALT	2 ML
¼ TSP	GRANULATED SUGAR	1 ML
2 TBSP	RICE VINEGAR OR CIDER VINEGAR	30 ML
3 TBSP	TOASTED SESAME SEEDS	45 ML
½ CUP	CREAM CHEESE, SOFTENED	125 ML
¼ CUP	MAYONNAISE	60 ML
1 TSP	SRIRACHA	5 ML
1	PACKAGE (7 OZ/200 G) IMITATION CRABMEAT, CHOPPED	1
1	AVOCADO, DICED	1
2 OZ	SMOKED SALMON, THINLY SLICED	60 G
6	PACKAGES (5 G EACH) KOREAN ROASTED SEAWEED SNACK	6
	SOY SAUCE	

IN A SAUCEPAN, BRING WATER TO BOIL. STIR IN RICE, SALT AND SUGAR. REDUCE HEAT TO LOW, COVER AND COOK FOR 20 MINUTES OR UNTIL WATER IS ABSORBED AND RICE IS TENDER. GENTLY STIR IN VINEGAR AND SCRAPE RICE MIXTURE INTO A PIE PLATE. SPRINKLE WITH SESAME SEEDS.

PREHEAT OVEN TO 350°F (180°C).

IN A BOWL, BEAT TOGETHER CREAM CHEESE, MAYONNAISE AND SRIRACHA. STIR IN CRABMEAT AND SPREAD OVER TOP OF THE RICE. COVER AND BAKE FOR ABOUT 25 MINUTES OR UNTIL HEATED THROUGH. SPRINKLE TOP WITH AVOCADO AND SMOKED SALMON. SPOON SUSHI BAKE ONTO NORI SHEETS TO SERVE. DRIZZLE WITH SOY SAUCE TO TASTE, IF DESIRED. SERVES 4 TO 6.

TIP: IF YOU LOVE SRIRACHA, INCREASE TO 2 TSP (10 ML) OR MORE IN THE CREAM CHEESE MIXTURE. NO AVOCADO? TRY $1/3$ CUP (75 ML) FINELY DICED CUCUMBER SPRINKLED OVER TOP FOR A REFRESHING TWIST.

SUBSTITUTE: FOR A BIG KICK OF HEAT, YOU CAN SUBSTITUTE 2 TBSP (30 ML) OF TOGARASHI SEASONING FOR THE SESAME SEEDS.

I EAT MY TACOS OVER A TORTILLA.
THAT WAY WHEN STUFF FALLS OUT,
BOOM, ANOTHER TACO.

HERB AND CHEESE BEEF ROLLS

"WE WOULDN'T CHANGE A THING" IS WHAT EMILY'S FRIENDS ANNETTE AND RAY SAID AFTER TASTING THESE LITTLE MORSELS. PERFECT APPETIZER, LIGHT LUNCH OR JUST ANOTHER EXCUSE TO EAT MORE CHEESE!

1/2 CUP	CREAM CHEESE, SOFTENED	125 ML
1/3 CUP	CRUMBLED FETA CHEESE	75 ML
2 TBSP	DICED RED BELL PEPPER	30 ML
1 TBSP	CHOPPED FRESH BASIL	15 ML
1/2 TSP	GRATED LEMON ZEST	2 ML
PINCH	EACH SALT AND BLACK PEPPER	PINCH
12	THIN SLICES RARE DELI ROAST BEEF	12
1 1/2 CUPS	BABY ARUGULA	375 ML
	BALSAMIC GLAZE	

IN A BOWL, BEAT TOGETHER CREAM CHEESE AND FETA CHEESE, RED PEPPER, BASIL, LEMON ZEST, SALT AND PEPPER. LAY BEEF SLICES ON WORK SURFACE AND DIVIDE CHEESE MIXTURE ONTO THE CENTER OF EACH SLICE. TOP WITH BABY ARUGULA AND ROLL UP. PLACE ON SERVING PLATTER AND DRIZZLE WITH BALSAMIC GLAZE TO SERVE. MAKES 12 ROLLS.

TIP: IN SOME DELIS YOU CAN FIND AIR-DRIED BEEF, KNOWN AS BRESAOLA. YOU CAN SUBSTITUTE IT FOR THE ROAST BEEF SLICES.

SALADS AND SANDWICHES

CARROT PARSLEY SALAD

*A TASTY ALTERNATIVE TO A GREEN SALAD,
THIS BRIGHT-COLORED SALAD MAINTAINS
A FRESH, ZESTY CRISPNESS THAT MAKES
IT PERFECT AS PART OF A PICNIC MEAL.*

2 TBSP	CANOLA OIL	30 ML
1 TBSP	CIDER VINEGAR	15 ML
2	GARLIC CLOVES, MINCED	2
2 TSP	LIQUID HONEY	10 ML
1/2 TSP	EACH SALT AND BLACK PEPPER	2 ML
1 LB	CARROTS (ABOUT 5 MEDIUM), GRATED	500 G
3 CUPS	LIGHTLY PACKED FRESH PARSLEY, COARSELY CHOPPED	750 ML
5	RADISHES, SLICED	5

IN A LARGE BOWL, COMBINE OIL, VINEGAR, GARLIC, HONEY, SALT AND PEPPER. ADD CARROTS, PARSLEY AND RADISHES AND TOSS TO COMBINE. ALLOW TO MARINATE 15 MINUTES BEFORE SERVING. SERVES 6.

MAKE AHEAD: SALAD CAN BE MADE AHEAD. COVER AND REFRIGERATE FOR UP TO 2 DAYS.

ARUGULA AVOCADO CITRUS SALAD

FRESH CITRUS, CREAMY RIPE AVOCADOS AND PEPPERY ARUGULA MAKE A WONDERFUL SALAD COMBINATION. COLLECT THE ZEST FROM ONE OF THE ORANGES BEFORE PREPARING THE ORANGE SEGMENTS FOR THE SALAD. WHEN PEELING THE ORANGES, BE SURE TO REMOVE AS MUCH OF THE WHITE PITH AS POSSIBLE.

1/4 CUP	CANOLA OIL	60 ML
2 TBSP	CIDER VINEGAR	30 ML
1	SHALLOT, THINLY SLICED	1
1 TSP	HONEY DIJON MUSTARD	5 ML
1/2 TSP	GRATED ORANGE ZEST	2 ML
1/2 TSP	EACH SALT AND BLACK PEPPER	2 ML
6 CUPS	BABY ARUGULA	1.5 L
4	ORANGES, PEELED AND SLICED INTO 1/2-INCH (1 CM) ROUNDS	4
2	AVOCADOS, PEELED AND SLICED	2
1/3 CUP	TOASTED PUMPKIN SEEDS	75 ML

IN A SMALL BOWL OR MASON JAR, WHISK OR SHAKE OIL, VINEGAR, SHALLOT, MUSTARD, ORANGE ZEST, SALT AND PEPPER TOGETHER; SET ASIDE. ARRANGE THE ARUGULA ON A PLATTER; ARRANGE THE ORANGES AND AVOCADOS ON TOP. DRIZZLE DRESSING OVER SALAD JUST BEFORE SERVING. SERVES 6.

MAKE AHEAD: PREPARE THE DRESSING AND THE ORANGES THE DAY BEFORE AND STORE IN AIRTIGHT CONTAINERS IN THE REFRIGERATOR.

GRILLED ASPARAGUS PANZANELLA SALAD

THIS COMBINATION OF TOMATOES AND BREAD IS
ENHANCED BY CRISP GRILLED SPEARS OF ASPARAGUS.
FEEL FREE TO GRILL UP THE WHOLE BUNCH
OF ASPARAGUS FOR MORE COLOR AND FLAVOR
AND ADD IT TO THE SALAD.

4	SLICES BREAD (SEE TIP)	4
1/4 CUP	EXTRA VIRGIN OLIVE OIL, DIVIDED	60 ML
1/2	BUNCH FRESH ASPARAGUS, TRIMMED	1/2
3 CUPS	GRAPE TOMATOES, HALVED	750 ML
3 TBSP	RED WINE VINEGAR	45 ML
1	GARLIC CLOVE, MINCED	1
1 TSP	DRIED OREGANO	5 ML
1/2 TSP	SALT	2 ML
PINCH	BLACK PEPPER	PINCH

PREHEAT GRILL TO MEDIUM-HIGH.

BRUSH BREAD WITH SOME OF THE OIL. TOSS
ASPARAGUS WITH A LITTLE OF THE OIL. PLACE BOTH ON
GREASED GRILL, TURNING OCCASIONALLY, FOR 4 MINUTES
OR UNTIL TOAST IS GOLDEN AND ASPARAGUS IS TENDER
BUT STILL CRISP. LET COOL SLIGHTLY.

CHOP BREAD INTO BITE-SIZE PIECES TO MAKE ABOUT
3 CUPS (750 ML); CHOP ASPARAGUS.

TOSS TOMATOES WITH REMAINING OIL, VINEGAR,
GARLIC AND OREGANO. STIR IN CHOPPED BREAD,

ASPARAGUS AND SALT AND PEPPER. LET SIT 10 MINUTES BEFORE SERVING FOR FLAVORS TO MARRY. SERVES 4 TO 6.

TIP: TASTE THE SALAD AFTER LETTING IT SIT FOR 10 MINUTES AND RE-SEASON IF NECESSARY.

TIP: USE A RUSTIC CRUSTY OVAL BREAD LOAF AND SLICE IT YOURSELF. MAKE THE SLICES ABOUT 1 INCH (2.5 CM) THICK. TRY OLIVE BREAD FOR ADDED FLAVOR.

FRESH HERB ADDITION: STIR IN $1/4$ CUP (60 ML) CHOPPED FRESH BASIL OR PARSLEY TO HEIGHTEN THAT SUMMER-FRESH FLAVOR.

SPOILER ALERT!
THE MILK HAS BEEN IN THE
FRIDGE FOR THREE WEEKS.

QUINOA SALAD WITH ROASTED TOMATOES AND FETA

CREAMY AVOCADO AND FETA COMBINED WITH FRESH HERBS AND CRUNCHY SEEDS GIVE THIS SALAD VARYING TEXTURES AND BRIGHT FLAVORS. QUINOA NEEDS A QUICK RINSE UNDER COLD RUNNING WATER TO WASH AWAY THE NATURAL COATING THAT CAN SOMETIMES TASTE BITTER.

3 CUPS	GRAPE TOMATOES, HALVED	750 ML
4	GARLIC CLOVES, MINCED	4
3 TBSP	CANOLA OIL, DIVIDED	45 ML
1/2 TSP	EACH SALT AND BLACK PEPPER	2 ML
I CUP	QUINOA, RINSED	250 ML
1 1/2 CUPS	WATER	375 ML
3 TBSP	LEMON JUICE	45 ML
2 TSP	GRATED LEMON ZEST	10 ML
1/2 TSP	GRANULATED SUGAR	2 ML
I	LARGE AVOCADO, PEELED AND CUBED	I
I CUP	CRUMBLED FETA CHEESE	250 ML
1 1/2 CUPS	CHOPPED FRESH PARSLEY	375 ML
I	GREEN ONION, SLICED	I
1/2 CUP	TOASTED PUMPKIN OR SUNFLOWER SEEDS	125 ML

PREHEAT OVEN TO 400°F (200°C); SET ASIDE A PARCHMENT PAPER LINED RIMMED BAKING SHEET. PLACE TOMATOES AND GARLIC ON BAKING SHEET AND TOSS WITH I TBSP (15 ML) OIL; SPRINKLE WITH SALT AND PEPPER.

BAKE 15 TO 20 MINUTES UNTIL TOMATOES ARE TENDER AND BEGINNING TO BROWN; SET ASIDE TO COOL.

MEANWHILE, IN A MEDIUM POT, PLACE QUINOA AND WATER OVER MEDIUM-HIGH HEAT, BRING TO A BOIL. COVER AND REDUCE HEAT TO SIMMER; COOK 10 MINUTES. REMOVE FROM HEAT, KEEP COVERED AND LET SIT 5 MINUTES. TRANSFER QUINOA TO A LARGE BOWL AND ADD REMAINING 2 TBSP (30 ML) OIL, LEMON JUICE, LEMON ZEST AND SUGAR, TOSSING TO COMBINE. GENTLY TOSS IN TOMATOES, GARLIC, AVOCADO, FETA, PARSLEY, GREEN ONION AND PUMPKIN SEEDS. SERVE RIGHT AWAY. SERVES 6.

MAKE AHEAD: TO GET A HEAD START ON THIS SALAD, COOK THE QUINOA AND ROAST THE TOMATOES AND GARLIC A DAY AHEAD. STORE IN THE REFRIGERATOR UNTIL READY TO ASSEMBLE SALAD.

GOING FOR A WALK BECAUSE I WANT TO STAY HEALTHY. TAKING ALONG A BOX OF M&MS BECAUSE, LET'S BE HONEST HERE.

FALAFEL SALAD
WITH TAHINI DRESSING

THERE'S NO NEED TO ROLL THE FALAFEL BALLS; SIMPLY SCOOP OUT AND BAKE. SERVE WITH PITA BREAD ON THE SIDE AND YOU'RE READY TO EAT!

FALAFEL

1	CAN (19 OZ/540 ML) CHICKPEAS, RINSED AND DRAINED	1
2	SHALLOTS, COARSELY CHOPPED	2
1/2 CUP	COARSELY CHOPPED FRESH PARSLEY	125 ML
2 TBSP	CORNSTARCH	30 ML
1 TBSP	ZA'ATAR SPICE MIX	15 ML
1/2 TSP	SALT	2 ML
2 TBSP	CANOLA OIL	30 ML

DRESSING

1/3 CUP	TAHINI	75 ML
1/4 CUP	LEMON JUICE	60 ML
2 TSP	MAPLE SYRUP	10 ML
1/4 TSP	GARLIC POWDER	1 ML
3/4 TSP	SALT	3 ML
3 TBSP	WARM WATER	45 ML

SALAD

8 CUPS	CHOPPED LETTUCE (SUCH AS ROMAINE OR GREEN LEAF)	2 L
2 CUPS	HALVED GRAPE TOMATOES	500 ML
1	ENGLISH CUCUMBER, SLICED	1
1/2	RED ONION, THINLY SLICED	1/2

PREHEAT OVEN TO 400°F (200°C); SET ASIDE AN OILED BAKING SHEET.

FALAFEL: IN A FOOD PROCESSOR, ADD CHICKPEAS, SHALLOTS, PARSLEY, CORNSTARCH, ZA'ATAR AND SALT. PULSE TO A CRUMBLY CONSISTENCY, UNTIL YOU CAN SQUEEZE A BALL THAT HOLDS TOGETHER AND DOESN'T STICK TO YOUR HANDS. (SCRAPE DOWN SIDES OF BOWL AS NEEDED.) IF MIXTURE IS TOO WET, ADD A LITTLE MORE CORNSTARCH. USING A MINI ICE CREAM SCOOP OR A TABLESPOON MEASURE, SCOOP MIXTURE (ABOUT 48 SMALL BALLS) ONTO PREPARED BAKING SHEET AND SLIGHTLY FLATTEN EACH BALL, THEN DRIZZLE WITH OIL. BAKE 25 MINUTES UNTIL GOLDEN BROWN AND CRISP.

DRESSING: MEANWHILE, IN A SMALL BOWL, WHISK TOGETHER TAHINI, LEMON JUICE, MAPLE SYRUP, GARLIC POWDER AND SALT; MIXTURE WILL BECOME VERY STIFF. ADD WATER AND CONTINUE WHISKING UNTIL MIXTURE IS WELL BLENDED AND CREAMY. ADD MORE WATER, I TSP (5 ML) AT A TIME, IF YOU PREFER THE DRESSING TO BE THINNER. REFRIGERATE UNTIL READY TO USE. MAKES ABOUT I CUP (250 ML).

SALAD: ARRANGE LETTUCE, TOMATOES, CUCUMBER, RED ONIONS AND FALAFEL ON A LARGE PLATTER OR 6 INDIVIDUAL PLATES. DRIZZLE WITH DRESSING JUST BEFORE SERVING. SERVES 6.

MAKE AHEAD: THE DRESSING CAN BE MADE AND REFRIGERATED FOR UP TO 5 DAYS. ADD WATER TO THIN DRESSING IF NEEDED.

TACO BEEF SALAD

YOU CAN USE THE HOMEMADE TACO SEASONING MIX ON PAGE 59 OR A STORE-BOUGHT MIX IN THIS CLASSIC RECIPE WITH A LENTIL TWIST. FEEL FREE TO ADD EXTRA TOPPINGS SUCH AS JALAPEÑOS AND AVOCADO TO CUSTOMIZE YOUR SALAD.

1 TSP	CANOLA OIL	5 ML
1 LB	LEAN GROUND BEEF	500 G
1 CUP	COOKED GREEN OR BROWN LENTILS	250 ML
3 TBSP	TACO SEASONING MIX (STORE-BOUGHT OR SEE RECIPE PAGE 59)	45 ML
4 CUPS	COLESLAW MIX	1 L
1	SMALL RED ONION, THINLY SLICED	1
1 CUP	SLICED GRAPE TOMATOES	250 ML
1/2 CUP	CORN KERNELS	125 ML
1 1/2 CUPS	SHREDDED TEX-MEX CHEESE	375 ML
	RANCH DRESSING	
	TACO CHIPS	

IN A LARGE NONSTICK SKILLET, HEAT OIL OVER MEDIUM-HIGH HEAT. ADD BEEF, LENTILS AND TACO SEASONING. COOK, STIRRING OCCASIONALLY, ABOUT 8 TO 10 MINUTES, OR UNTIL MEAT IS COOKED THROUGH. DRAIN OFF ANY EXCESS FAT IF NECESSARY. REMOVE FROM HEAT AND ALLOW TO COOL A FEW MINUTES.

IN A LARGE BOWL, COMBINE COLESLAW, ONION, TOMATOES, CORN AND CHEESE AND BEEF. ADD DRESSING, TO TASTE. SERVE WITH TACO CHIPS. SERVES 4.

HOMEMADE TACO SEASONING MIX

IT TAKES ONLY MINUTES TO MAKE A BATCH OF THIS VERSATILE SPICE MIX. USE TO FLAVOR RICE OR SPRINKLE ON SOUP, POPCORN OR GRILLED MEAT. YOU CAN USE THIS MIX IN SEVERAL OF OUR RECIPES SUCH AS TACO BEEF SALAD, PAGE 58, CHORIZO AND BLACK BEANS ON RICE, PAGE 140, AND SMOKY SALMON BOWL, PAGE 156.

2 TBSP	CHILI POWDER	30 ML
2 TBSP	SMOKED PAPRIKA	30 ML
1 TBSP	CORNSTARCH	15 ML
1 TBSP	GARLIC POWDER	15 ML
1 TBSP	DRIED OREGANO	15 ML
1 TBSP	ONION POWDER	15 ML
2 TSP	GROUND CUMIN	10 ML
1 TSP	EACH SALT AND BLACK PEPPER	5 ML
$1/2$ TSP	GRANULATED SUGAR	2 ML

IN A SMALL JAR, COMBINE ALL INGREDIENTS. STORE IN A COOL PLACE FOR UP TO 3 MONTHS. MAKES $1/2$ CUP (125 ML).

CAULIFLOWER "POTATO" SALAD

*TAKE THE CLASSIC AND CHANGE IT UP BY
USING CAULIFLOWER INSTEAD OF POTATOES!*

1	LARGE HEAD CAULIFLOWER, LEAVES REMOVED	1
1 CUP	LIGHT MAYONNAISE	250 ML
2 TBSP	CIDER VINEGAR	30 ML
1 TBSP	DIJON MUSTARD	15 ML
1/2 TSP	CELERY SEED	2 ML
1/2 TSP	SALT	2 ML
1/4 TSP	BLACK PEPPER	1 ML
2	CELERY STALKS, DICED	2
3	GREEN ONIONS, THINLY SLICED	3
3 TBSP	CHOPPED FRESH PARSLEY	45 ML
2	HARD-COOKED EGGS, CHOPPED	2
2	BABY DILL PICKLES, CHOPPED	2

CUT CAULIFLOWER INTO LARGE PIECES TO GET ABOUT
8 CUPS (2 L). COOK IN POT OF BOILING WATER FOR
ABOUT 8 MINUTES OR UNTIL TENDER. DRAIN WELL AND
RINSE WITH COLD WATER; LET DRAIN AND BREAK INTO
BITE-SIZE PIECES.

IN A LARGE BOWL, WHISK TOGETHER MAYONNAISE,
VINEGAR, MUSTARD, CELERY SEED, SALT AND PEPPER. STIR
IN CELERY, ONIONS AND PARSLEY. ADD CAULIFLOWER AND
STIR GENTLY TO COAT. ADD EGGS AND PICKLES AND STIR
TO DISTRIBUTE. COVER AND REFRIGERATE FOR AT LEAST
1 HOUR OR UP TO 24 HOURS BEFORE SERVING. SERVES 8.

TOMATO AND HARISSA CREAM CHEESE TOASTS

CRUNCHY, CREAMY AND SLIGHTLY SPICY, THESE TOASTS ARE SIMPLE TO MAKE AND DELICIOUS. SALTING THE TOMATOES IN ADVANCE IMPROVES THEIR FLAVOR.

4	PLUM (ROMA) TOMATOES	4
1/4 TSP	SALT	1 ML
4 OZ	BRICK-STYLE CREAM CHEESE (1/2 BRICK), SOFTENED	125 G
1 1/2 TSP	HARISSA PASTE (OR 3/4 TSP/3 ML HARISSA SPICE)	7 ML
4	LARGE SLICES HEARTY BREAD, TOASTED	4
1/4 CUP	CHOPPED FRESH CILANTRO	60 ML
	EXTRA VIRGIN OLIVE OIL	
	BLACK PEPPER	

SLICE TOMATOES AND SPRINKLE WITH SALT; LET SIT 5 MINUTES, THEN DRAIN ANY JUICES.

MEANWHILE, IN A MEDIUM BOWL, COMBINE CREAM CHEESE AND HARISSA PASTE. SPREAD MIXTURE ONTO BREAD, LAYER TOMATOES ON TOP AND SPRINKLE WITH CILANTRO. DRIZZLE WITH A LITTLE OIL AND SPRINKLE WITH PEPPER. SERVES 4.

TIP: HARISSA IS A NORTH AFRICAN SPICE MIX THAT INCLUDES A VARIETY OF CHILE PEPPERS AND SPICES SUCH AS CARAWAY, CORIANDER SEEDS AND CUMIN SEEDS. YOU CAN FIND HARISSA IN THE SPICE AISLE AS A PASTE OR AS A DRIED MIX IN A JAR.

GRILLED VEGETABLE PANINI WITH MINTED MAYO

THIS COLORFUL SANDWICH IS FULL OF GRILLED VEGETABLES THAT WILL MAKE YOU WANT TO SAVOR EACH BITE. FOR A VEGAN TWIST, LOOK FOR VEGAN MAYONNAISE FOR THE MAYO SPREAD.

2	RED BELL PEPPERS, QUARTERED	2
2	YELLOW BELL PEPPERS, QUARTERED	2
2	PORTOBELLO MUSHROOMS, STEMS REMOVED	2
2	ZUCCHINI, SLICED LENGTHWISE	2
1/4 CUP	EXTRA VIRGIN OLIVE OIL	60 ML
1/4 CUP	RED WINE VINEGAR	60 ML
1/2 TSP	DIJON MUSTARD	2 ML
1	GARLIC CLOVE, MINCED	1
1/2 TSP	EACH SALT AND BLACK PEPPER	2 ML
1/2 CUP	MAYONNAISE	125 ML
2 TBSP	CHOPPED FRESH MINT	30 ML
4	SOFT KAISER BUNS, CUT IN HALF	4

IN A LARGE BOWL, COMBINE RED AND YELLOW PEPPERS, MUSHROOMS AND ZUCCHINI.

PREHEAT GRILL TO MEDIUM-HIGH HEAT.

IN A SMALL BOWL, WHISK TOGETHER OIL, VINEGAR, MUSTARD, GARLIC, SALT AND PEPPER. POUR ALL BUT 2 TBSP (30 ML) OVER VEGETABLES AND TOSS TO COAT WELL.

PLACE VEGETABLES ON GREASED GRILL; CLOSE LID AND GRILL, TURNING ONCE, FOR ABOUT 12 MINUTES OR UNTIL TENDER. REMOVE TO THE SAME LARGE BOWL. CUT MUSHROOMS INTO THICK SLICES.

IN A SMALL BOWL, WHISK TOGETHER MAYONNAISE AND MINT. ADD RESERVED 2 TBSP (30 ML) OF THE OIL MIXTURE. SPREAD OVER CUT SIDES OF BUNS. LAYER THE VEGETABLES INTO THE BUNS TO SERVE. SERVES 4.

TIP: FOR A LIGHTER-COLORED MUSHROOM AND GREAT FLAVOR, USE A SMALL SPOON TO SCRAPE OUT THE GILLS OF THE MUSHROOMS BEFORE ADDING THEM TO THE BOWL BEFORE GRILLING.

MAKE AHEAD: GRILL ALL THE VEGETABLES THE DAY BEFORE SO ALL YOU HAVE TO DO IS PUT THE SANDWICH TOGETHER. YOU CAN MAKE THE MAYONNAISE MIXTURE AHEAD AS WELL.

TIP: FOR A TOASTED BUN, BEFORE PUTTING THE SANDWICH TOGETHER, PLACE THE CUT BUNS ON THE GRILL UNTIL GRILL-MARKED.

ROAST PEPPER CHEESE STROMBOLI ROLLS

THIS VEGETARIAN CHEESE STROMBOLI IS GREAT TO HAVE ON HAND IN THE FRIDGE TO POP IN THE MICROWAVE OR OVEN TO REHEAT.

1½ LB	PIZZA OR BREAD DOUGH	750 G
1	TUB (1 LB/500 G) RICOTTA CHEESE	1
3	LARGE EGGS	3
1 CUP	CHOPPED ROASTED RED BELL PEPPERS	250 ML
½ CUP	FRESHLY GRATED PARMESAN CHEESE	125 ML
2 TBSP	CHOPPED FRESH ITALIAN PARSLEY	30 ML
¼ TSP	EACH SALT AND BLACK PEPPER	1 ML
1 TBSP	EXTRA VIRGIN OLIVE OIL	15 ML

PREHEAT OVEN TO 400°F (200°C); SET ASIDE A PARCHMENT PAPER LINED BAKING SHEET. CUT DOUGH INTO 6 EQUAL PIECES. ON FLOURED SURFACE, ROLL OUT EACH PIECE TO ABOUT 6- BY 8-INCH (15 BY 20 CM) RECTANGLES.

IN A LARGE BOWL, STIR TOGETHER RICOTTA CHEESE, EGGS, ROASTED PEPPERS, CHEESE, PARSLEY, SALT AND PEPPER. SPOON ABOUT ½ CUP (125 ML) OF MIXTURE EVENLY ONTO EACH PIECE OF DOUGH. GENTLY ROLL UP AND PLACE ON PREPARED BAKING SHEET. BRUSH WITH OIL.

BAKE IN BOTTOM THIRD OF OVEN FOR ABOUT 25 MINUTES OR UNTIL CRUST IS GOLDEN AND FILLING IS SET. SERVES 6.

TIP: BE SURE TO DRAIN THE ROASTED PEPPERS WELL AND PAT DRY BEFORE ADDING THEM TO THE MIXTURE, TO NOT ADD MORE MOISTURE.

TIP: CHANGE UP THE FILLING AND ADD OTHER ROASTED OR COOKED VEGETABLES FOR THE PEPPERS. FOR AN ADDED GOOEY TEXTURE, ADD $\frac{1}{2}$ CUP (125 ML) SHREDDED MOZZARELLA CHEESE TO THE FILLING.

TIP: LOOKING TO SERVE WITH A SAUCE? USE SALSA OR PIZZA SAUCE AS A DIP.

PIZZA SLIDERS

WHAT'S NOT TO LOVE ABOUT THESE DELICIOUS SANDWICH BUNS WITH A CRISPY EXTERIOR AND A MELTY CHEESE AND PEPPERONI INSIDE? THESE SLIDERS ARE EASY TO PREPARE AND CAN BE MADE AHEAD OF TIME.

1/4 CUP	BUTTER	60 ML
2 TSP	DRIED ITALIAN SEASONING, DIVIDED	10 ML
1/2 TSP	GARLIC POWDER	2 ML
1/2 TSP	ONION POWDER	2 ML
1	TRAY 12 DINNER ROLLS	1
1 CUP	PIZZA SAUCE	250 ML
2 CUPS	SHREDDED MOZZARELLA, DIVIDED	500 ML
1 1/2 CUPS	SLICED MINI PEPPERONI (ABOUT 6 OZ/175 G)	375 ML
1/4 CUP	SHREDDED PARMESAN CHEESE	60 ML

PREHEAT OVEN TO 400°F (200°C); SET ASIDE A LIGHTLY GREASED OR PARCHMENT PAPER LINED BAKING SHEET. IN A SMALL POT, OVER MEDIUM HEAT, MELT BUTTER. REMOVE FROM HEAT, THEN STIR IN 1 TSP (5 ML) OF THE ITALIAN SEASONING, GARLIC POWDER AND ONION POWDER; SET ASIDE.

LEAVE ROLLS ATTACHED AND SLICE IN HALF HORIZONTALLY. (IT'S OKAY IF A FEW COME APART.) PLACE THE BOTTOM HALF ON PREPARED BAKING SHEET AND SPREAD PIZZA SAUCE EVENLY ON TOP. SPRINKLE WITH HALF THE MOZZARELLA CHEESE AND THE REMAINING 1 TSP (5 ML) ITALIAN SEASONING. LAYER THE PEPPERONI ON TOP AND SPRINKLE WITH REMAINING MOZZARELLA.

REPLACE THE TOP HALF OF THE ROLLS AND BRUSH HALF OF THE BUTTER MIXTURE OVER THE TOP AND SIDES OF THE ROLLS. COVER LOOSELY WITH FOIL, BAKE 13 MINUTES. REMOVE FOIL, BRUSH WITH REMAINING BUTTER MIXTURE AND SPRINKLE PARMESAN CHEESE ON TOP. BAKE UNCOVERED FOR 5 MINUTES, UNTIL THE ROLLS ARE GOLDEN BROWN ON TOP. SERVES 8 TO 12.

TIP: IF YOU ARE UNABLE TO FIND TRAY BUNS, USE 12 BRIOCHE OR OTHER SMALL DINNER ROLLS.

MAKE AHEAD: THIS RECIPE CAN BE PARTIALLY ASSEMBLED AHEAD OF TIME. PROCEED WITH RECIPE TO THE STEP OF BRUSHING THE SLIDERS WITH HALF OF THE BUTTER MIXTURE. COVER TIGHTLY AND REFRIGERATE UP TO ONE DAY AHEAD.

TIP: IF YOU LIKE A LITTLE EXTRA HEAT, USE HOT PEPPERONI OR SPRINKLE ABOUT 1 TSP (5 ML) RED PEPPER FLAKES ON THE BOTTOM HALF OF THE BUNS BEFORE PUTTING THE TOP BACK ON.

SEAFOOD DINNER ROLL SANDWICH

FOR SOME ADDED CRUNCH TO THIS SANDWICH, TRY CRUSHING YOUR FAVORITE POTATO CHIPS OVER TOP BEFORE TAKING A BITE — YOU MAY NEVER REGRET IT. DILL PICKLE CHIPS MAKE A WINNER TOPPING, IN OUR OPINION.

3 TBSP	BUTTER	45 ML
2	GREEN ONIONS, THINLY SLICED	2
1	CELERY STALK, FINELY CHOPPED	1
1/2	RED BELL PEPPER, DICED	1/2
8 OZ	SMALL COOKED SHRIMP	250 G
1	CAN (6 OZ/170 G) CHUNK LIGHT TUNA, DRAINED	1
1	CAN (4 1/4 OZ/120 G) CRABMEAT, DRAINED	1
1/2 CUP	MAYONNAISE, DIVIDED	125 ML
1 TSP	OLD BAY SEASONING	5 ML
1/4 TSP	SALT	1 ML
PINCH	BLACK PEPPER	PINCH
6	SOFT HOTDOG BUNS, SPLIT	6
6	LEMON WEDGES (OPTIONAL)	6

IN A SKILLET, MELT BUTTER OVER MEDIUM-HIGH HEAT AND COOK GREEN ONIONS, CELERY AND RED PEPPER FOR 5 MINUTES TO SOFTEN. STIR IN SHRIMP AND COOK, STIRRING FOR ABOUT 2 MINUTES OR UNTIL SHRIMP IS HEATED. REMOVE FROM HEAT AND STIR IN TUNA,

CRABMEAT, HALF OF THE MAYONNAISE, SEASONING, SALT AND PEPPER UNTIL WELL COMBINED.

SPREAD REMAINING MAYONNAISE AMONG BUNS AND PLACE ON BAKING SHEET. TOAST IN 400°F (200°C) OVEN FOR 5 MINUTES. DIVIDE SEAFOOD MIXTURE AMONG BUNS AND RETURN TO OVEN FOR ABOUT 3 MINUTES TO WARM THROUGH. SERVE WITH LEMON WEDGE, IF DESIRED. SERVES 6.

HOT STUFF: EMILY'S LONGTIME FRIEND CHRIS LOVES SOME HEAT IN HIS SANDWICH AND SUGGESTED ADDING 1 JALAPEÑO PEPPER, SEEDED AND MINCED, TO THE GREEN ONION MIXTURE TO COOK, OR ADD A FEW SPLASHES OF YOUR FAVORITE HOT SAUCE TO THE MIXTURE BEFORE FILLING THE BUNS.

TIP: CHANGE UP THE BREAD AND TRY SERVING IT ON KAISER BUNS OR SMALLER DINNER ROLLS FOR A SLIDER OPTION.

TIP: IF YOU CAN'T FIND OLD BAY SEASONING (LOOK IN THE SPICE AISLE OR THE FISH DEPARTMENT AT YOUR GROCERY STORE), YOU CAN SUBSTITUTE 1/2 TSP (2 ML) CELERY SALT.

GRILLED SCALOPPINE SANDWICH WITH PICKLED VEGETABLE MAYO

CRUNCHY PICKLED GARDEN VEGETABLES ARE A REFRESHING TOPPING FOR THIS SANDWICH. GRILLING SCALOPPINE IS FAST AND MAKES A HEARTY SANDWICH. LOOK FOR PICKLED VEGETABLES IN THE GROCERY AISLE WHERE PICKLES AND OLIVES ARE SOLD.

PICKLED VEGETABLE MAYO

I CUP	CHOPPED DRAINED PICKLED MIXED VEGETABLES (MILD OR HOT)	250 ML
1/3 CUP	LIGHT MAYONNAISE	75 ML
I TBSP	CHOPPED FRESH PARSLEY	15 ML
I	GARLIC CLOVE, MINCED	I
PINCH	BLACK PEPPER	PINCH

GRILLED SCALOPPINE

4	TURKEY OR CHICKEN SCALOPPINE (ABOUT 12 OZ/375 G TOTAL)	4
I TBSP	CANOLA OIL	15 ML
I TSP	DRIED OREGANO	5 ML
I TSP	DRIED BASIL LEAVES	5 ML
1/4 TSP	EACH SALT AND BLACK PEPPER	I ML
4	SMALL SUB BUNS, HALVED	4
2 CUPS	SHREDDED LETTUCE	500 ML
I	TOMATO, THINLY SLICED	I

PICKLED VEGETABLE MAYO: IN A BOWL, STIR TOGETHER VEGETABLES, MAYONNAISE, PARSLEY, GARLIC AND PEPPER UNTIL COMBINED; SET ASIDE.

GRILLED SCALOPPINE: PREHEAT GRILL TO MEDIUM-HIGH HEAT. IN A BOWL, TOSS TURKEY WITH OIL, OREGANO, BASIL, SALT AND PEPPER. PLACE ON GREASED GRILL OVER MEDIUM-HIGH HEAT, TURNING ONCE, FOR ABOUT 6 MINUTES OR UNTIL NO LONGER PINK INSIDE. SPRINKLE BUNS WITH LETTUCE AND TOP WITH GRILLED SCALOPPINE AND TOMATO. SPREAD EACH WITH PICKLED VEGETABLE MAYO. SERVES 4.

SKILLET OPTION: YOU CAN COOK THE SCALOPPINE IN A NONSTICK SKILLET OVER MEDIUM-HIGH HEAT FOR ABOUT 8 MINUTES, TURNING ONCE.

TIP: IF YOU NEED TO MAKE YOUR OWN SCALOPPINE, USE BONELESS SKINLESS TURKEY OR CHICKEN AND SLICE CROSSWISE INTO THIN CUTLETS. IF NECESSARY, POUND THEM OUT TO ABOUT A $\frac{1}{4}$-INCH (5 MM) THICKNESS.

SRIRACHA EGG SALAD SANDWICHES

WE LOVE A TWIST ON A SIMPLE CLASSIC. THE EGG FILLING GETS A LITTLE CRUNCH FROM THE CELERY AND A FLAVOR KICK WITH ONE OF OUR FAVORITE INGREDIENTS — SRIRACHA!

1/3 CUP	MAYONNAISE	75 ML
1 TSP	GRAINY MUSTARD	5 ML
1 TBSP	SRIRACHA	15 ML
1 TSP	CIDER VINEGAR	5 ML
1/2 TSP	EACH SALT AND BLACK PEPPER	2 ML
8	HARD-COOKED EGGS, PEELED AND COARSELY CHOPPED	8
3	CELERY STALKS, FINELY DICED	3
2	GREEN ONIONS, FINELY CHOPPED	2
3 TBSP	CHOPPED FRESH CILANTRO	45 ML
8	SLICES TOASTED BREAD	8

IN A MEDIUM BOWL, COMBINE MAYONNAISE, MUSTARD, SRIRACHA, VINEGAR, SALT AND PEPPER; STIR TO COMBINE. ADD EGGS, CELERY, GREEN ONIONS AND CILANTRO; GENTLY STIR TO COMBINE. TASTE AND ADD MORE SRIRACHA IF DESIRED. SPOON ONTO BREAD TO MAKE SANDWICHES. SERVES 4.

TIP: FILLING CAN BE MADE AHEAD, COVERED AND REFRIGERATED FOR UP TO 3 DAYS.

SOUPS

SUCCOTASH SOUP

USE FRESH AND FROZEN VEGETABLES TO
CREATE THIS EASY, COLORFUL SOUP FROM A
COMBINATION THAT IS TRADITIONALLY A SIDE DISH.
NO SUFFERING SUCCOTASH HERE.

2 TBSP	CANOLA OIL	30 ML
1	SMALL ONION, DICED	1
1 CUP	SMALL DICED SQUASH (SUCH AS BUTTERNUT)	250 ML
2	GARLIC CLOVES, MINCED	2
1/2 TSP	SALT	2 ML
2 CUPS	FRESH OR FROZEN CORN KERNELS	500 ML
1 CUP	FROZEN LIMA BEANS, SHELLED EDAMAME OR CHOPPED GREEN BEANS	250 ML
1	SMALL RED BELL PEPPER, DICED	1
4 CUPS	READY-TO-USE VEGETABLE BROTH	1 L
1/4 CUP	CHOPPED FRESH BASIL	60 ML
	BLACK PEPPER	

IN A SOUP POT, HEAT OIL OVER MEDIUM HEAT AND COOK
ONION, SQUASH, GARLIC AND SALT FOR ABOUT 5 MINUTES
OR UNTIL ONIONS HAVE SOFTENED. ADD CORN, BEANS AND
RED PEPPER, STIRRING TO COAT. ADD BROTH AND BRING TO
A BOIL. COVER AND SIMMER FOR 10 MINUTES. STIR IN BASIL
AND SEASON TO TASTE WITH PEPPER. SERVES 4 TO 6.

QUICK BLACK BEAN SOUP

THIS RECIPE HITS THE SPOT WHEN YOU'RE CRAVING
A BOWL OF HOT SOUP THAT'S THICK AND FLAVORFUL.
THERE'S NO NEED TO DRAIN THE CANS OF BEANS,
AS THE LIQUID IS PART OF THE SOUP. SERVE WITH
CORNBREAD, A BISCUIT OR RICE ON THE SIDE.

1 TBSP	CANOLA OIL	15 ML
1	ONION, FINELY CHOPPED	1
4	GARLIC CLOVES, MINCED	4
2 TSP	CHILI POWDER	10 ML
1 TSP	GROUND CUMIN	5 ML
2	CANS (19 OZ/540 ML) BLACK BEANS, UNDRAINED	2
4 CUPS	READY-TO-USE CHICKEN BROTH	1 L
1 CUP	CHOPPED FRESH CILANTRO, DIVIDED	250 ML
1/4 CUP	LIME JUICE	60 ML

IN A LARGE POT, OVER MEDIUM-HIGH HEAT, HEAT OIL
AND ADD ONION. COOK, STIRRING OCCASIONALLY FOR
4 MINUTES. ADD GARLIC, CHILI POWDER AND CUMIN AND
COOK 30 SECONDS. ADD BEANS (INCLUDING LIQUID),
CHICKEN BROTH AND HALF OF THE CILANTRO. BRING TO A
BOIL, THEN COVER AND REDUCE HEAT TO MEDIUM-LOW
AND SIMMER 15 MINUTES. STIR IN REMAINING CILANTRO
AND LIME JUICE. IF YOU LIKE A CREAMIER SOUP, USE A
POTATO MASHER OR IMMERSION BLENDER TO PUREÉ
SOME OF THE BEANS TO DESIRED TEXTURE. SERVES 4.

TIP: STORE IN THE REFRIGERATOR FOR UP TO 4 DAYS OR
FREEZE FOR UP TO 2 MONTHS.

SMOKY RED LENTIL SOUP

THIS SATISFYING AND HEARTY SOUP IS
PERFECT FOR DAYS WHEN YOU'RE SHORT ON TIME.
JUST BEFORE COOKING, PLACE MEASURED LENTILS
IN A COLANDER AND RINSE WITH COLD WATER
TO REMOVE ANY DUST OR DEBRIS.

2 TBSP	CANOLA OIL	30 ML
1	ONION, FINELY CHOPPED	1
3	CARROTS, FINELY CHOPPED	3
2 CUPS	DRIED SPLIT RED LENTILS	500 ML
1	CAN (28 OZ/796 ML) CRUSHED TOMATOES	1
8 CUPS	READY-TO-USE CHICKEN BROTH	2 L
3	GARLIC CLOVES, MINCED	3
2 TBSP	SMOKED PAPRIKA	30 ML
1 TSP	GROUND CUMIN	5 ML
2 TSP	BALSAMIC VINEGAR	10 ML
	SALT AND BLACK PEPPER	
1/3 CUP	CHOPPED FRESH CILANTRO OR PARSLEY	75 ML
	SOUR CREAM	

IN A LARGE POT, HEAT OIL OVER MEDIUM-HIGH HEAT.
ADD ONION AND CARROTS AND SAUTÉ FOR 5 MINUTES,
STIRRING OCCASIONALLY UNTIL VEGETABLES BEGIN TO
SOFTEN. STIR IN LENTILS, TOMATOES, BROTH, GARLIC,
PAPRIKA AND CUMIN. BRING TO A BOIL, REDUCE HEAT TO
MEDIUM-LOW, COVER AND SIMMER FOR 12 TO 15 MINUTES,
UNTIL LENTILS ARE TENDER AND SOUP HAS THICKENED.

STIR IN VINEGAR AND SEASON TO TASTE WITH SALT AND PEPPER. SERVE GARNISHED WITH CILANTRO AND A DOLLOP OF SOUR CREAM. SERVES 8.

TIP: YOU CAN SUBSTITUTE VEGETABLE BROTH FOR THE CHICKEN BROTH.

MAKE AHEAD: THIS SOUP FREEZES WELL FOR UP TO 2 MONTHS.

SORRY, I JUST SAW YOUR TEXT FROM LAST NIGHT. ARE YOU GUYS STILL AT THE RESTAURANT?

CREAMY MUSHROOM SOUP

THIS SIMPLE SOUP IS LOADED WITH MUSHROOM
FLAVOR. YOU CAN DECIDE IF YOU WANT IT SMOOTH
OR CHUNKY, SO CHANGE IT UP ONCE IN A WHILE.

2 TBSP	BUTTER	30 ML
I LB	BUTTON MUSHROOMS, SLICED	500 G
I LB	CREMINI MUSHROOMS, SLICED	500 G
I	SMALL ONION, DICED	I
2	GARLIC CLOVES, MINCED	2
2 TSP	CHOPPED FRESH THYME (I TSP/5 ML DRIED THYME)	IO ML
4 CUPS	READY-TO-USE VEGETABLE OR CHICKEN BROTH	I L
I CUP	HEAVY OR WHIPPING (35%) CREAM	250 ML
I TSP	SALT	5 ML
	FRESH THYME SPRIGS (OPTIONAL)	

IN A SOUP POT, HEAT BUTTER OVER MEDIUM-HIGH HEAT
AND COOK MUSHROOMS, ONION, GARLIC AND THYME,
STIRRING OFTEN FOR ABOUT 20 MINUTES OR UNTIL
GOLDEN AND LIQUID EVAPORATES. ADD BROTH, CREAM
AND SALT; BRING TO A BOIL AND SIMMER GENTLY FOR
IO MINUTES. USING AN IMMERSION BLENDER, BLEND SOUP
UNTIL SMOOTH. LADLE SOUP INTO BOWLS AND GARNISH
WITH FRESH THYME SPRIGS, IF DESIRED. SERVES 4.

TIP: FOR A SMOOTHER SOUP, PURÉE SOUP IN BATCHES IN
BLENDER AND RETURN TO SOUP POT TO HEAT THROUGH.
FOR A RUSTIC-STYLE SOUP, DO NOT PURÉE.

TIP: YOU CAN USE A VARIETY OF MUSHROOMS, INCLUDING SHIITAKE AND OYSTER MUSHROOMS, FOR THE SOUP. A COMBINATION OF THEM ALL WILL GIVE YOU A WONDERFUL FLAVOR.

CHEESE VARIATION: STIR IN $\frac{1}{2}$ CUP (125 ML) FRESHLY GRATED PARMESAN CHEESE INTO THE SOUP. YOU CAN ALSO SIMPLY GARNISH EACH BOWL WITH SHREDDED OLD (SHARP) CHEDDAR CHEESE AND STIR IT IN YOURSELF!

TIP: IF YOU HAVE A PARMESAN RIND HANDY, BE SURE TO ADD THAT TO SOUP WHILE IT'S SIMMERING FOR EVEN MORE CHEESE FLAVOR.

CHICKPEA CAULIFLOWER SOUP

THIS COMBINATION WILL HELP YOU FIND ANOTHER REASON TO BUY CAULIFLOWER AGAIN! BY PUREÉING THE SOUP YOU END UP WITH A SMOOTH TEXTURE AND A HINT OF GINGER AND CUMIN THAT TASTES GREAT.

1 TBSP	CANOLA OIL	15 ML
1	ONION, CHOPPED	1
2	GARLIC CLOVES, MINCED	2
1	CARROT, CHOPPED	1
1	CELERY STALK, CHOPPED	1
1 TBSP	MINCED FRESH GINGER	15 ML
1 TBSP	GROUND CUMIN	15 ML
3/4 TSP	GROUND CORIANDER	3 ML
1/2 TSP	GROUND TURMERIC	2 ML
1/4 TSP	CAYENNE PEPPER (OPTIONAL)	1 ML
6 CUPS	CHOPPED CAULIFLOWER	1.5 L
2	CANS (19 OZ/540 ML EACH) CHICKPEAS, RINSED AND DRAINED	2
6 CUPS	READY-TO-USE VEGETABLE OR CHICKEN BROTH	1.5 L
1/2 TSP	SALT	2 ML
1/2 CUP	BALKAN-STYLE OR GREEK PLAIN YOGURT	125 ML
3 TBSP	CHOPPED FRESH CILANTRO	45 ML

IN A SOUP POT, HEAT OIL OVER MEDIUM HEAT AND COOK ONION, GARLIC, CARROT, CELERY, GINGER, CUMIN, CORIANDER, TURMERIC AND CAYENNE (IF USING) FOR 5 MINUTES OR UNTIL SOFTENED AND FRAGRANT.

ADD CAULIFLOWER AND CHICKPEAS AND COOK, STIRRING FOR 2 MINUTES OR UNTIL COATED. ADD BROTH AND SALT; BRING TO A BOIL. COVER AND SIMMER FOR ABOUT 20 MINUTES OR UNTIL CAULIFLOWER IS TENDER.

USE AN IMMERSION BLENDER OR TRANSFER SOUP TO BLENDER OR FOOD PROCESSOR IN BATCHES AND PURÉE UNTIL SMOOTH. RETURN TO SOUP POT AND REHEAT UNTIL STEAMING.

SERVE SOUP WITH DOLLOP OF YOGURT AND SPRINKLE OF CILANTRO. SERVES 6 TO 8.

MAKE AHEAD: ONCE THE SOUP IS COMPLETELY COOL YOU CAN STORE IT IN AIRTIGHT CONTAINERS AND FREEZE FOR UP TO 1 MONTH OR KEEP REFRIGERATED FOR UP TO 3 DAYS.

TIP: YOU WILL NEED TO BUY 1 SMALL HEAD OF CAULIFLOWER, ABOUT $1\frac{1}{2}$ LB (750 G), TO GET 6 CUPS (1.5 L) OF CHOPPED CAULIFLOWER.

SATAY TOFU NOODLE SOUP

SO DELICIOUS AND SLURP-WORTHY, THIS NOODLE SOUP
EXPLODES WITH FLAVOR AND TEXTURE. ADD MORE CURRY
PASTE IF YOU ENJOY YOUR SOUP EXTRA SPICY.

12 OZ	FLAT RICE NOODLES	375 G
2 TSP	CANOLA OIL	10 ML
3	GARLIC CLOVES, MINCED	3
1 TBSP	GRATED FRESH GINGER	15 ML
3/4 CUP	CREAMY PEANUT BUTTER	175 ML
1 TBSP	THAI RED CURRY PASTE	15 ML
3 TBSP	SOY SAUCE	45 ML
2 TBSP	TOMATO PASTE	30 ML
10 CUPS	READY-TO-USE CHICKEN BROTH	2.5 L
12 OZ	FIRM TOFU, DRAINED AND CUBED	375 G
3 CUPS	BEAN SPROUTS	750 ML
1/2 CUP	LIGHTLY PACKED FRESH THAI OR SWEET BASIL LEAVES	125 ML
1/3 CUP	CHOPPED ROASTED PEANUTS	75 ML
	LIME WEDGES	

PLACE NOODLES IN A LARGE BOWL AND COVER WITH HOT
WATER; LET SOAK FOR 15 MINUTES, OR UNTIL AL DENTE.
DRAIN AND SET ASIDE.

MEANWHILE, IN A LARGE POT, OVER MEDIUM HEAT, HEAT
OIL, ADD GARLIC AND GINGER AND COOK, STIRRING, FOR
30 SECONDS. STIR IN PEANUT BUTTER, CURRY PASTE,
SOY SAUCE, TOMATO PASTE AND COOK FOR 30 SECONDS.
INCREASE HEAT TO MEDIUM-HIGH HEAT, ADD BROTH

AND BRING TO A SIMMER. COVER AND REDUCE HEAT TO MEDIUM; COOK 10 MINUTES. ADD TOFU AND COOK 1 MINUTE, THEN STIR IN BEAN SPROUTS AND REMOVE FROM HEAT. DIVIDE NOODLES INTO SIX LARGE SOUP BOWLS. LADLE SOUP INTO EACH BOWL AND TOP WITH BASIL AND PEANUTS. SERVE LIME WEDGES ON THE SIDE. SERVES 6.

TIP: PEANUTS CAN GO RANCID VERY QUICKLY. STORE IN THE REFRIGERATOR OR FREEZER AND GIVE THEM A QUICK TASTE TEST BEFORE USING.

THE NEXT TIME YOU HAVE COMPANY,
SERVE THEM A BOWL OF SHELLED PEANUTS.
AFTER THEY'VE EATEN A FEW HANDFULS,
CASUALLY MENTION THAT YOU'VE NEVER LIKED
PEANUTS, BUT YOU LOVE TO SUCK
THE SALT OFF OF THEM.

SPAGHETTI AND MEATBALL SOUP

THIS ONE-POT HEARTY SOUP WILL NEED SPOONS AND FORKS. IT'S A FAMILY FAVORITE WITH A TWIST.

1 LB	GROUND CHICKEN OR TURKEY	500 G
1/3 CUP	CHOPPED FRESH ITALIAN PARSLEY	75 ML
1/3 CUP	FRESHLY GRATED PARMESAN CHEESE	75 ML
1	GARLIC CLOVE, MINCED	1
PINCH	SALT	PINCH
PINCH	HOT PEPPER FLAKES	PINCH
8 CUPS	READY-TO-USE CHICKEN BROTH	2 L
1	JAR (22 OZ/650 ML) TOMATO AND BASIL PASTA SAUCE	1
12 OZ	WHITE SPAGHETTI ENRICHED WITH FIBER	375 G
	FRESHLY GRATED PARMESAN CHEESE (OPTIONAL)	

IN A LARGE BOWL, COMBINE GROUND CHICKEN, PARSLEY, CHEESE, GARLIC, SALT AND PEPPER FLAKES WITH YOUR HANDS UNTIL WELL MIXED. USING ABOUT 1 TBSP (15 ML) OF THE MIXTURE AT A TIME, MAKE SMALL MEATBALLS AND PLACE ON A PLATE.

IN A LARGE SOUP POT, BRING CHICKEN BROTH AND PASTA SAUCE TO A GENTLE BOIL. BREAK SPAGHETTI IN HALF, IN SMALL BUNCHES, AND ADD TO POT, STIRRING OCCASIONALLY FOR 3 MINUTES. ADD MEATBALLS AND

COOK FOR ABOUT 6 MINUTES OR UNTIL PASTA IS TENDER BUT FIRM AND MEATBALLS ARE NO LONGER PINK INSIDE. GARNISH BOWLS WITH MORE PARMESAN, IF DESIRED. SERVES 6.

TIP: ENJOY THIS SOUP IMMEDIATELY TO KEEP ITS SOUP-LIKE CONSISTENCY. AS IT SITS THE SPAGHETTI ABSORBS THE BROTH AND BECOMES THICK. IT IS STILL DELICIOUS, BUT YOU MAY NOT NEED THAT SPOON LATER WITH LEFTOVERS.

TIP: IF YOU ARE FEEDING LITTLE ONES IN THE FAMILY, FEEL FREE TO BREAK THE SPAGHETTI INTO SMALLER PIECES BEFORE ADDING IT TO THE SOUP. CLEANUP WILL BE MUCH EASIER.

MY WIFE IS ON A TROPICAL FRUIT DIET — THE HOUSE IS FULL OF THE STUFF! IT'S ENOUGH TO MAKE A MANGO CRAZY.

TURKEY BARLEY SOUP

THIS HEARTY SOUP WILL WARM YOU UP ON A COLD WINTER'S NIGHT. IT'S COMFORT FOOD THAT WARMS THE SOUL AND FEEDS THE BELLY. ADD A SPLASH OF HOT SAUCE FOR AN EXTRA KICK OF SPICE IN EACH BOWL.

1 TBSP	CANOLA OIL	15 ML
1 LB	GROUND TURKEY	500 G
1	ONION, CHOPPED	1
2	GARLIC CLOVES, MINCED	2
8 OZ	BUTTON MUSHROOMS, SLICED	250 G
1	CARROT, CHOPPED	1
1	CELERY STALK, CHOPPED	1
1 TSP	DRIED THYME	5 ML
2 TBSP	TOMATO PASTE	30 ML
1/2 TSP	EACH SALT AND BLACK PEPPER	2 ML
1/2 CUP	BARLEY	125 ML
7 CUPS	READY-TO-USE CHICKEN OR VEGETABLE BROTH	1.75 L
1	BAY LEAF	1

IN A SOUP POT, HEAT OIL OVER MEDIUM-HIGH HEAT AND BROWN TURKEY. REDUCE HEAT TO MEDIUM AND ADD ONION AND GARLIC; COOK, STIRRING FOR 3 MINUTES. ADD MUSHROOMS, CARROT, CELERY AND THYME; COOK, STIRRING, FOR 10 MINUTES. STIR IN TOMATO PASTE, SALT AND PEPPER TO COAT. STIR IN BARLEY AND POUR IN BROTH AND BAY LEAF. COVER AND BRING TO A BOIL. REDUCE HEAT TO A GENTLE SIMMER. SIMMER FOR ABOUT

30 MINUTES OR UNTIL BARLEY IS TENDER. REMOVE BAY LEAF BEFORE SERVING. SERVES 6

TIP: A SPRINKLE OF FRESHLY GRATED PARMESAN CHEESE ADDS A DELICIOUS TOUCH TO THIS SOUP. OR IF YOU HAVE A SMALL RIND OF PARMESAN CHEESE, ADD IT WHEN YOU ADD THE BROTH FOR A WONDERFUL ADDITION OF FLAVOR.

MAKE AHEAD: YOU CAN MAKE THE SOUP THE NIGHT BEFORE BUT WILL NEED TO ADD MORE BROTH WHEN HEATING IT UP, AS THE BARLEY SOAKS UP ALL THAT GREAT FLAVOR! ADD 1 TO 2 CUPS (250 TO 500 ML) MORE BROTH WHEN HEATING THE SOUP.

JUSTICE IS A DISH BEST SERVED COLD — BECAUSE IF IT WERE SERVED WARM, IT WOULD BE JUSTWATER.

BUFFALO CHICKEN CHOWDER

THIS HEARTY AND SPICY CHOWDER IS PREPARED IN THE INSTANT POT. A STEAMING BOWL OF THIS SOUP WILL LEAVE YOU FEELING TOASTY AND WARM. IF DESIRED, TOP WITH CRUMBLED BLUE CHEESE OR SHREDDED CHEDDAR FOR THAT CLASSIC FLAVOR COMBINATION.

1 TBSP	CANOLA OIL	15 ML
1	ONION, CHOPPED	1
1½ LB	BONELESS, SKINLESS CHICKEN THIGHS	750 G
4	CELERY STALKS, CHOPPED	4
3	CARROTS, CHOPPED	3
3	POTATOES, UNPEELED AND CHOPPED	3
3 CUPS	READY-TO-USE CHICKEN BROTH	750 ML
⅓ CUP	HOT PEPPER SAUCE (SUCH AS FRANK'S REDHOT)	75 ML
1 TSP	GARLIC POWDER	5 ML
1 CUP	HALF AND HALF (10%) CREAM	250 ML
3 TBSP	CORNSTARCH	45 ML
3	GREEN ONIONS, SLICED	3

IN A 6-QUART INSTANT POT, PRESS SAUTÉ AND ADD OIL AND ONION TO THE POT. COOK, STIRRING OCCASIONALLY, ABOUT 3 MINUTES, UNTIL ONION BEGINS TO SOFTEN AND BROWN. ADD CHICKEN, CELERY, CARROTS, POTATOES, BROTH, HOT SAUCE AND GARLIC POWDER; STIR TO COMBINE. PRESS CANCEL AND LOCK LID; SET PRESSURE RELEASE VALVE TO SEALING. PRESS MANUAL PRESSURE COOK; SET TO HIGH FOR 10 MINUTES. (IT TAKES ABOUT

10 MINUTES TO COME TO PRESSURE.) WHEN COOKING
FINISHES, ALLOW THE PRESSURE TO RELEASE NATURALLY
FOR 15 MINUTES, THEN RELEASE ANY REMAINING STEAM
BY MOVING THE PRESSURE RELEASE VALVE TO VENTING.
PRESS CANCEL; OPEN LID.

REMOVE CHICKEN TO A PLATE OR CUTTING BOARD
AND SHRED USING TWO FORKS, THEN RETURN CHICKEN
TO POT. IN A SMALL BOWL, COMBINE CREAM AND
CORNSTARCH; STIR INTO POT. SELECT SAUTÉ AND COOK,
STIRRING 2 MINUTES, OR UNTIL CHOWDER THICKENS AND
BUBBLES. STIR IN GREEN ONIONS. SERVE WITH EXTRA
HOT SAUCE ON THE SIDE. SERVES 6 TO 8.

TIP: THIS CHOWDER CAN BE STORED IN THE REFRIGERATOR
FOR UP TO 3 DAYS

SAUSAGE POTATO SOUP WITH GREENS

THIS HEARTY SOUP, ALSO KNOWN AS CALDO VERDE, IS FILLED WITH GREENS AND SAVORY CHORIZO SAUSAGE AND IS A FAVORITE FOR MANY. TRY USING DIFFERENT GREENS TO CHANGE UP THE FLAVOR; RAPINI, COLLARDS OR SPINACH ALL WORK REALLY WELL.

2 TBSP	CANOLA OIL, DIVIDED	30 ML
8 OZ	SEMI-CURED READY-TO-EAT SWEET OR MILD CHORIZO SAUSAGE, SLICED	250 G
1	LARGE SWEET ONION, CHOPPED	1
2	CELERY STALKS, CHOPPED	2
1	LARGE CARROT, CHOPPED	1
4	GARLIC CLOVES, MINCED	4
1/4 TSP	HOT PEPPER FLAKES	1 ML
8 CUPS	CHOPPED KALE LEAVES OR CHOPPED SWISS CHARD	2 L
1 LB	POTATOES (ABOUT 2 LARGE), CHOPPED	500 G
2	BAY LEAVES	2
6 CUPS	READY-TO-USE CHICKEN OR VEGETABLE BROTH	1.5 L
	SALT AND BLACK PEPPER	

IN A LARGE SOUP POT, HEAT 1 TBSP (15 ML) OF THE OIL OVER MEDIUM HEAT AND SAUTÉ SAUSAGE ABOUT 3 MINUTES OR UNTIL BROWNED. REMOVE TO BOWL.

RETURN POT TO HEAT; ADD REMAINING OIL. COOK ONION, CELERY, CARROT, GARLIC AND HOT PEPPER FLAKES FOR ABOUT 5 MINUTES OR UNTIL SOFTENED. STIR IN KALE

UNTIL WILTED. ADD POTATOES, BROWNED SAUSAGE AND BAY LEAVES, STIRRING TO COAT. POUR IN BROTH AND BRING TO A BOIL. COVER AND SIMMER GENTLY FOR ABOUT 15 MINUTES OR UNTIL POTATO IS TENDER. REMOVE BAY LEAVES BEFORE SERVING AND SEASON TO TASTE WITH SALT AND PEPPER. SERVES 6 TO 8.

TIP: WANT TO CHANGE THIS UP A BIT? WHY NOT TRY SWEET POTATO FOR THE REGULAR POTATOES — OR MIX THEM UP? EMILY'S FRIEND PAOLA LOVES TO ADD SOME COLOR TO THIS WONDERFUL SOUP THIS WAY.

FOR HALLOWEEN WE DRESSED UP
AS ALMONDS. EVERYONE COULD
TELL WE WERE NUTS.

CHICKEN TURMERIC RICE SOUP

WE LOVE THIS SATISFYING, FLAVORFUL VERSION OF CHICKEN SOUP. THE TURMERIC ADDS A BEAUTIFUL GOLDEN COLOR AND AN EARTHY SWEET TASTE.

1 TBSP	CANOLA OIL	15 ML
3	CARROTS, DICED	3
2	CELERY STALKS, DICED	2
4	GARLIC CLOVES, MINCED	4
2 TSP	GROUND TURMERIC	10 ML
1 TSP	GROUND GINGER	5 ML
1 CUP	LONG-GRAIN RICE	250 ML
6 CUPS	READY-TO-USE CHICKEN BROTH	1.5 L
2 CUPS	DICED COOKED CHICKEN	500 ML
2 CUPS	LIGHTLY PACKED BABY SPINACH	500 ML
1 TBSP	LEMON JUICE	15 ML
	SALT AND BLACK PEPPER	

IN A LARGE POT, OVER MEDIUM-HIGH HEAT, HEAT OIL. ADD CARROTS AND CELERY; COOK, STIRRING OCCASIONALLY, FOR 5 MINUTES. ADD GARLIC, TURMERIC, GINGER AND RICE; COOK, STIRRING, FOR 30 SECONDS. ADD BROTH, SCRAPING UP ANY COOKED BITS FROM THE BOTTOM OF THE POT, AND BRING TO SIMMER. REDUCE HEAT TO MEDIUM, COVER AND COOK 15 TO 20 MINUTES, OR UNTIL RICE IS TENDER. STIR IN CHICKEN, SPINACH AND LEMON JUICE; COVER AND SIMMER 5 MINUTES OR UNTIL HEATED THROUGH. SEASON TO TASTE WITH SALT AND PEPPER. SERVES 8.

MAKE AHEAD: DICE THE CARROTS AND CELERY, COVER AND REFRIGERATE FOR UP TO 2 DAYS.

BEEF AND VEAL

BEEF AND LENTIL MEATLOAF

THIS JUICY AND TENDER MEATLOAF IS
DELICIOUS AS A SANDWICH FILLING.

1 1/2 LB	LEAN GROUND BEEF OR VEAL	750 G
1 CUP	COOKED GREEN OR BROWN LENTILS	250 ML
3/4 CUP	DRY BREAD CRUMBS	175 ML
3/4 CUP	BARBECUE SAUCE, DIVIDED	175 ML
2	LARGE EGGS, LIGHTLY BEATEN	2
1 TSP	DRIED ITALIAN SEASONING	5 ML
1/2 TSP	GARLIC POWDER	2 ML
1/2 TSP	ONION POWDER	2 ML
1/2 TSP	BLACK PEPPER	2 ML

PREHEAT OVEN TO 375°F (190°C); SET ASIDE A 9- BY 5-INCH
(23 BY 12.5 CM) LOAF PAN. IN A LARGE BOWL, COMBINE
BEEF, LENTILS, BREAD CRUMBS, 1/4 CUP (60 ML) BARBECUE
SAUCE, EGGS, ITALIAN SEASONING, GARLIC POWDER, ONION
POWDER AND PEPPER. MIX GENTLY UNTIL WELL COMBINED;
LIGHTLY PACK INTO LOAF PAN. SPOON THE REMAINING
1/2 CUP (125 ML) BARBECUE SAUCE OVER THE TOP AND BAKE
ABOUT 50 MINUTES, OR UNTIL NO LONGER PINK INSIDE
AND AN INSERTED MEAT THERMOMETER REGISTERS
160°F (71°C). LET STAND 10 MINUTES BEFORE SLICING AND
SERVING. SERVES 6.

MAKE AHEAD: ASSEMBLE THE MEATLOAF AND PLACE IN
PAN; COVER AND REFRIGERATE TO BAKE THE NEXT DAY.

TIP: DOUBLE THE RECIPE — EAT ONE LOAF AND FREEZE
THE OTHER FOR A FUTURE MEAL.

SPINACH FETA MINI MEATLOAVES

BAKING THE MEATLOAVES IN A MUFFIN PAN SPEEDS UP COOKING TIME. LEFTOVERS CAN BE TUCKED INTO A BUN OR PITA BREAD FOR A QUICK MEAL ON THE GO.

1½ LB	LEAN GROUND BEEF OR VEAL	750 G
1 CUP	LIGHTLY PACKED SPINACH, CHOPPED	250 ML
½ CUP	QUICK-COOKING ROLLED OATS	125 ML
½ CUP	CRUMBLED FETA CHEESE	125 ML
¼ CUP	CHOPPED BLACK OLIVES	60 ML
¼ CUP	SUN-DRIED TOMATOES, FINELY CHOPPED	60 ML
1	LARGE EGG, LIGHTLY BEATEN	1
1½ TSP	DRIED OREGANO	7 ML
1 TSP	GARLIC POWDER	5 ML

PREHEAT OVEN TO 400°F (200°C). PLACE A 12-CUP MUFFIN PAN ON A RIMMED BAKING SHEET TO CATCH ANY DRIPS WHILE BAKING. IN A LARGE BOWL, ADD BEEF, SPINACH, OATS, FETA, OLIVES, SUN-DRIED TOMATOES, EGG, OREGANO AND GARLIC POWDER; MIX GENTLY UNTIL WELL COMBINED. DIVIDE MEAT MIXTURE EVENLY AMONG MUFFIN CUPS. (AN ICE CREAM SCOOP IS HELPFUL.) BAKE 20 TO 25 MINUTES, OR UNTIL A MEAT THERMOMETER INSERTED IN THE CENTER OF A MINI MEATLOAF REGISTERS AT LEAST 160°F (71°C). SERVES 6.

MAKE AHEAD: PREPARE MEATLOAVES AND REFRIGERATE IN MUFFIN PAN TO BAKE THE NEXT DAY.

TIP: YOU CAN USE EITHER SUN-DRIED TOMATOES IN OIL OR DRY-PACK SUN-DRIED TOMATOES FOR THIS RECIPE.

BEEF-STUFFED FLATBREAD

THIS RECIPE IS INSPIRED BY GÖZLEME,
A SAVORY FILLED TURKISH FLATBREAD.

2 TSP	CANOLA OIL, DIVIDED	10 ML
1	ONION, FINELY CHOPPED	1
1 LB	LEAN GROUND BEEF OR VEAL	500 G
2	GARLIC CLOVES, MINCED	2
2 TBSP	TOMATO PASTE	30 ML
1 TBSP	GROUND CUMIN	15 ML
1/2 TSP	EACH SALT AND BLACK PEPPER	2 ML
3 CUPS	LIGHTLY PACKED SPINACH	750 ML
1 1/2 CUPS	CRUMBLED FETA CHEESE	375 ML
4	10-INCH (25 CM) FLOUR TORTILLAS	4

IN A LARGE SKILLET, OVER MEDIUM-HIGH HEAT, HEAT 1 TSP OIL. ADD ONION AND COOK, STIRRING OCCASIONALLY, FOR 4 MINUTES. ADD BEEF AND GARLIC; COOK, STIRRING FOR 7 MINUTES, UNTIL MEAT IS BROWNED AND COOKED. STIR IN TOMATO PASTE, CUMIN, SALT AND PEPPER; COOK FOR 2 MINUTES. REMOVE FROM HEAT AND STIR IN SPINACH UNTIL WILTED. COOL MIXTURE FOR 10 MINUTES; STIR IN FETA.

DIVIDE MIXTURE ONTO EACH TORTILLA; FOLD OVER TO ENCLOSE FILLING. IN A LARGE SKILLET, OVER MEDIUM HEAT, HEAT REMAINING 1 TSP (5 ML) OIL. PLACE 2 FILLED TORTILLAS INTO SKILLET AND FRY FOR ABOUT 3 MINUTES PER SIDE UNTIL CRISPY. REPEAT WITH REMAINING TORTILLAS, ADDING MORE OIL IF NECESSARY. SERVES 4.

French Toast Sticks with Maple Orange Dip (page 16)

Blender Zucchini Muffins (page 20)

Edamame Lemon Hummus (page 43)

Pam's Herb and Shallot–Marinated Shrimp (page 44)

Arugula Avocado Citrus Salad (page 51)

Quinoa Salad with Roasted Tomatoes and Feta (page 54)

Grilled Vegetable Panini with Minted Mayo (page 62)

Smoky Red Lentil Soup (page 76)

CHEESEBURGER PIE

TAKE YOUR FAVORITE BURGER LOADED WITH CHEESE AND FORGET THE BUN — USE PASTRY INSTEAD! DON'T FORGET THE KETCHUP, MUSTARD AND RELISH.

1¼ LB	LEAN GROUND BEEF OR VEAL	625 G
¼ TSP	EACH SALT AND BLACK PEPPER	1 ML
1 CUP	SHREDDED CHEDDAR CHEESE	250 ML
⅓ CUP	MAYONNAISE	75 ML
1	PACKAGE (14 OZ/400 G) REFRIGERATED PIE CRUSTS	1
4	SLICES PROCESSED CHEESE	4
½ CUP	SLICED PICKLES	125 ML
1	LARGE EGG, LIGHTLY BEATEN	1

IN A SKILLET, COOK BEEF, SALT AND PEPPER OVER MEDIUM-HIGH HEAT FOR ABOUT 8 MINUTES OR UNTIL NO LONGER PINK INSIDE. DRAIN FAT, IF ANY. STIR IN SHREDDED CHEESE AND MAYONNAISE TO COMBINE.

PREHEAT OVEN TO 375°F (190°C). LAY 1 PIE CRUST INTO A 9-INCH (23 CM) PIE PLATE. SPOON HALF OF THE BEEF FILLING INTO THE PIE CRUST BOTTOM. TOP WITH CHEESE SLICES AND PICKLES. SPOON REMAINING BEEF OVER TOP. LAY REMAINING PIE CRUST OVER TOP AND PINCH AROUND EDGES TO SEAL. BRUSH TOP WITH EGG AND CUT A FEW VENT SLASHES IN THE TOP OF THE PIE.

BAKE FOR 30 TO 40 MINUTES OR UNTIL PASTRY IS GOLDEN BROWN. LET COOL SLIGHTLY BEFORE CUTTING TO SERVE. SERVES 4 TO 6.

BACON AND MUSHROOM-
STUFFED FAMILY BURGER

WHEN ONE BURGER WILL BE ENOUGH TO FEED THE
FAMILY, YOU WANT IT TO BE THE BEST ONE AND TASTE
GREAT, TOO. NO BUN NEEDED, BUT ROASTED POTATOES
AND VEGETABLES ARE PERFECT ACCOMPANIMENTS.

8 OZ	BACON SLICES, CHOPPED	250 G
8 OZ	SLICED MUSHROOMS	250 G
1 1/2 LB	LEAN GROUND BEEF OR VEAL	750 G
3 TBSP	BASIL PESTO OR SUN-DRIED TOMATO PESTO	45 ML
1	GARLIC CLOVE, MINCED	1
1/2 TSP	EACH SALT AND BLACK PEPPER	2 ML
1	LARGE EGG, LIGHTLY BEATEN	1
1/3 CUP	FRESH BREAD CRUMBS	75 ML

PREHEAT OVEN TO 375°F (190°C). SET ASIDE A PARCHMENT
PAPER LINED BAKING SHEET. IN A SKILLET, COOK BACON
AND MUSHROOMS OVER MEDIUM-HIGH HEAT FOR ABOUT
15 MINUTES OR UNTIL BACON IS CRISPY AND MUSHROOMS
ARE GOLDEN. DRAIN FAT, IF ANY, AND SET ASIDE.

IN A LARGE BOWL, USING YOUR HANDS, MIX TOGETHER
BEEF, PESTO, GARLIC, SALT, PEPPER, EGG AND BREAD
CRUMBS UNTIL EVENLY COMBINED.

DIVIDE MEAT MIXTURE IN HALF AND SHAPE ONE HALF
INTO AN 8-INCH (20 CM) PATTY. PLACE IT ON PREPARED
BAKING SHEET AND PRESS GENTLY IN CENTER, LEAVING

A 1-INCH (2.5 CM) EDGE AROUND PATTY. PLACE BACON AND MUSHROOMS INTO CENTER CAVITY OF THE PATTY. PRESS OUT REMAINING HALF INTO A SIMILAR SIZE PATTY AND PLACE OVER TOP OF BACON AND MUSHROOM FILLING. PINCH TOGETHER AND SHAPE PATTY TOGETHER INTO A LARGE BURGER.

BAKE FOR ABOUT 25 MINUTES OR UNTIL NO LONGER PINK INSIDE. LET COOL SLIGHTLY BEFORE SLICING INTO WEDGES TO ENJOY. SERVES 4.

CHEESE VARIATION: STIR IN $\frac{1}{2}$ CUP (125 ML) SHREDDED CHEESE INTO BACON AND MUSHROOM MIXTURE FOR A GOOEY INTERIOR.

WHY DO SEAGULLS FLY OVER THE SEA? BECAUSE IF THEY FLEW OVER THE BAY THEY'D BE BAGELS!

FRENCH DIP BEEF PAN SLIDERS

THESE ARE A FAVORITE FOR FAMILIES WHO LOVE WATCHING THE GAME WITH HEARTY SNACKS OR JUST WANT TO ENJOY GOOD FOOD WITH FRIENDS. THEY'RE EASY TO MAKE AND EVEN EASIER TO ENJOY.

HORSERADISH CREAM

2 TBSP	SOUR CREAM	30 ML
2 TBSP	MAYONNAISE	30 ML
1 TBSP	HORSERADISH	15 ML
PINCH	BLACK PEPPER	PINCH

FRENCH DIP BEEF SLIDERS

3 TBSP	BUTTER	45 ML
1	LARGE SWEET ONION, THINLY SLICED	1
1/2 TSP	GRANULATED SUGAR	2 ML
2 TBSP	BALSAMIC VINEGAR	30 ML
1/2 TSP	CHOPPED FRESH THYME	2 ML
2 1/2 CUPS	READY-TO-USE BEEF BROTH	625 ML
1 LB	THINLY SLICED RARE DELI ROAST BEEF	500 G
12	MINI BRIOCHE BUNS, HALVED	12
1 TSP	WORCESTERSHIRE SAUCE	5 ML
1	SMALL GARLIC CLOVE, RASPED	1
1 1/2 CUPS	SHREDDED MOZZARELLA-CHEDDAR CHEESE BLEND	375 ML

HORSERADISH CREAM: IN A SMALL BOWL, WHISK TOGETHER SOUR CREAM, MAYONNAISE, HORSERADISH AND PEPPER; SET ASIDE.

FRENCH DIP BEEF SLIDERS: PREHEAT OVEN TO 400°F (200°C). SET ASIDE A BAKING SHEET.

IN A SKILLET, MELT BUTTER OVER MEDIUM-LOW HEAT. ADD ONION AND SUGAR; COOK, STIRRING OCCASIONALLY FOR 10 MINUTES OR UNTIL STARTING TO SOFTEN. CONTINUE TO COOK, STIRRING OFTEN FOR ABOUT 5 MINUTES OR UNTIL VERY SOFT AND GOLDEN. STIR IN VINEGAR AND THYME AND COOK FOR 2 MINUTES OR UNTIL VINEGAR IS ABSORBED; REMOVE FROM HEAT. IN A SAUCEPAN, BRING BEEF BROTH TO A GENTLE SIMMER. ADD ROAST BEEF TO HEAT THROUGH.

SPREAD BOTTOM HALVES OF SLIDER BUNS WITH HORSERADISH CREAM AND PLACE ON THE BAKING SHEET. DIVIDE ONIONS AMONG BOTTOM HALVES OF BUNS. USING TONGS, REMOVE ROAST BEEF FROM BROTH, LETTING DRAIN WELL (TO PREVENT SOGGY SANDWICHES), AND ADD TO SLIDERS.

STIR IN WORCESTERSHIRE SAUCE AND GARLIC INTO BROTH; LET SIMMER FOR 2 MINUTES.

MEANWHILE, SPRINKLE BEEF WITH CHEESE AND PLACE TOP HALVES OF BUNS ON SLIDERS. PLACE SLIDERS IN OVEN FOR ABOUT 5 MINUTES TO TOAST BUNS AND MELT CHEESE. WHEN READY, SERVE WITH BROTH MIXTURE TO DIP SLIDERS INTO. SERVES 4 TO 6.

TIP: IF ANYONE HAS FISH ALLERGIES, BE SURE TO REPLACE THE WORCESTERSHIRE WITH SOY SAUCE.

TIP: USE A RASP OR THE FINE SIDE OF A CHEESE GRATER FOR YOUR GARLIC CLOVE.

OVEN STEAK
WITH ASPARAGUS

SOMETIMES YOU JUST DON'T WANT TO PAY ATTENTION TO DINNER, SO THE SHEET-PAN MEAL IS PERFECT FOR THIS. STICK IT IN THE OVEN AND HAVE A DRINK WHILE YOU RELAX AND WAIT. DING! SEE, THAT WAS THE TIMER — DINNER'S READY. YOU'RE WELCOME.

2	BEEF GRILLING STEAKS (ABOUT 1 INCH/2.5 CM THICK)	2
2 TBSP	CANOLA OIL	30 ML
$\frac{1}{2}$ TSP	EACH SALT AND BLACK PEPPER	2 ML
1	BUNCH ASPARAGUS, CUT INTO 2-INCH (5 CM) PIECES	1
2 TBSP	BUTTER, MELTED	30 ML

PLACE RIMMED BAKING SHEET INTO A COLD OVEN. TURN OVEN TO 500°F (250°C) AND LET PAN WARM UP UNTIL TEMPERATURE IS REACHED.

MEANWHILE, PAT STEAKS DRY WITH PAPER TOWEL. CUT INTO 1-INCH (2.5 CM) CUBES AND TOSS WITH OIL, SALT AND PEPPER TO COAT. USING OVEN MITTS, REMOVE BAKING SHEET FROM OVEN. ADD STEAK AND ASPARAGUS, AND RETURN TO OVEN FOR 8 MINUTES OR UNTIL STEAK IS MEDIUM RARE OR DESIRED DONENESS. DRIZZLE WITH BUTTER TO SERVE. SERVES 4.

SUN-DRIED TOMATO OIL AND HERB GRILLED STEAK

GET AN EXTRA ZIP OF FLAVOR BY RUBBING THE STEAKS IN THE PARSLEY AND GARLIC MIXTURE AFTER THEY ARE GRILLED. THIS IS SIMPLE AND SO TASTY.

2 TBSP	SUN-DRIED TOMATO OIL OR EXTRA VIRGIN OLIVE OIL	30 ML
1/2 TSP	DRIED ITALIAN SEASONING	2 ML
1/4 TSP	EACH SALT AND BLACK PEPPER	1 ML
2	BEEF STRIPLOIN OR RIBEYE STEAK (ABOUT 1 LB/500 G TOTAL)	2
2 TBSP	CHOPPED FRESH PARSLEY	30 ML
1 TBSP	FINELY CHOPPED SUN-DRIED TOMATOES IN OIL	15 ML
1	GARLIC CLOVE, MINCED	1

IN A SHALLOW DISH, STIR TOGETHER SUN-DRIED TOMATO OIL, ITALIAN SEASONING, SALT AND PEPPER. ADD STEAKS AND TURN WELL TO COAT; LET STAND FOR 15 MINUTES. PREHEAT GRILL TO MEDIUM-HIGH.

PLACE STEAKS ON GREASED GRILL AND GRILL FOR ABOUT 6 MINUTES, TURNING ONCE, OR UNTIL DESIRED DONENESS.

MIX PARSLEY, SUN-DRIED TOMATOES AND GARLIC TOGETHER ON CUTTING BOARD AND PLACE STEAKS ON TOP. RUB BOTH SIDES OF THE STEAKS INTO THE HERB AND GARLIC MIXTURE. LET STAND FOR 3 MINUTES BEFORE SLICING THINLY TO SERVE. SERVES 4.

SOY LIME BEEF AND PEPPER SKEWERS

TENDER CUBES OF BEEF ARE MARINATED TO SOAK UP A WONDERFUL FLAVOR THAT BALANCES PERFECTLY WITH THE SWEET PEPPERS.

1/3 CUP	SOY SAUCE	75 ML
3 TBSP	LIME OR LEMON JUICE	45 ML
2 TBSP	PACKED BROWN SUGAR	30 ML
2 TBSP	CANOLA OIL	30 ML
1/4 TSP	EACH SALT AND BLACK PEPPER	1 ML
3	GARLIC CLOVES, MINCED	3
1 1/2 LB	STRIPLOIN STEAK, CUT INTO 1 1/2-INCH (4 CM) CUBES	750 G
1	RED BELL PEPPER, CUT INTO 1 1/2-INCH (4 CM) PIECES	1
1	YELLOW BELL PEPPER, CUT INTO 1 1/2-INCH (4 CM) PIECES	1
	FLAT METAL SKEWERS OR SOAKED BAMBOO SKEWERS	

IN A LARGE BOWL OR RESEALABLE BAG, COMBINE SOY SAUCE, LIME JUICE, BROWN SUGAR, OIL, SALT, PEPPER AND GARLIC. STIR IN BEEF, COATING WELL. COVER AND REFRIGERATE FOR AT LEAST 4 HOURS OR UP TO 12 HOURS.

PREHEAT BARBECUE GRILL TO HIGH. THREAD ALTERNATING PIECES OF BEEF AND VEGETABLES ONTO SKEWERS; DISCARD MARINADE. GRILL SKEWERS, TURNING ONCE, FOR 5 MINUTES FOR MEDIUM-RARE OR TO DESIRED DONENESS. SERVES 4 TO 6.

CHICKEN AND TURKEY

LEMONGRASS CHICKEN WITH NOODLES

KICK UP THE FLAVOR OF PASTA WITH THIS EASY CHICKEN DISH. LEMONGRASS PASTE IS A HANDY CONVENIENCE INGREDIENT THAT IS AVAILABLE IN TUBES OR FROZEN IN CUBES.

12 OZ	DRIED SPAGHETTI OR LINGUINE	375 G
2 TBSP	CANOLA OIL	30 ML
I LB	LEAN GROUND CHICKEN	500 G
3	GARLIC CLOVES, MINCED	3
3	GREEN ONIONS, SLICED	3
3 TBSP	LEMONGRASS PASTE OR MINCED LEMONGRASS	45 ML
3 TBSP	FISH SAUCE	45 ML
2 TBSP	LIME JUICE	30 ML
2 TBSP	PACKED BROWN SUGAR	30 ML
2 TSP	SRIRACHA	IO ML
4 CUPS	FROZEN ASIAN VEGETABLE MIX, THAWED SLIGHTLY	I L
3/4 CUP	LIGHTLY PACKED FRESH BASIL LEAVES	175 M

IN A LARGE POT OF BOILING SALTED WATER, COOK PASTA ABOUT 8 TO IO MINUTES UNTIL AL DENTE. DRAIN PASTA, TRANSFER BACK TO POT AND COVER TO KEEP WARM.

MEANWHILE, IN A LARGE SKILLET, HEAT OIL OVER MEDIUM-HIGH HEAT AND ADD CHICKEN. COOK 5 MINUTES, USING A WOODEN SPOON TO BREAK MEAT APART. STIR IN THE GARLIC, GREEN ONIONS, LEMONGRASS, FISH SAUCE,

LIME JUICE, BROWN SUGAR, SRIRACHA AND FROZEN VEGETABLES; COOK 7 MINUTES, OR UNTIL CHICKEN IS COOKED THROUGH AND VEGETABLES ARE TENDER CRISP. TRANSFER MIXTURE INTO POT OF PASTA, ADD BASIL LEAVES; TOSS TO FULLY COAT PASTA IN SAUCE. SERVES 5.

TIP: TO USE FRESH LEMONGRASS, USE THE WHITE BULB PORTION (ABOUT 6 INCHES/15 CM). CUT OFF THE TOUGH ROOT END AND REMOVE A FEW OF THE TOUGH OUTER LAYERS. LIGHTLY SMASH LEMONGRASS WITH THE FLAT PART OF A KNIFE OR WITH A ROLLING PIN, THEN FINELY CHOP.

TIP: FEEL FREE TO USE THAI BASIL IN PLACE OF REGULAR BASIL IN THIS RECIPE.

MY WIFE MADE ME A GREEN HAMBURGER TODAY TO CELEBRATE ST. PATRICK'S DAY. I ASKED HER HOW SHE COLORED IT AND SHE SAID SHE DIDN'T KNOW WHAT I WAS TALKING ABOUT.

TURKEY ZUCCHINI MEATBALLS

THE ADDITION OF ZUCCHINI KEEPS THESE EASY MEATBALLS TENDER AND JUICY. SERVE ON TOP OF ZUCCHINI NOODLES OR PASTA OR A COMBINATION OF THE TWO, ALONG WITH A GARNISH OF GRATED PARMESAN AND HOT PEPPER FLAKES, IF DESIRED.

I LB	LEAN GROUND TURKEY	500 G
I CUP	GRATED ZUCCHINI	250 ML
3/4 CUP	DRY BREAD CRUMBS	175 ML
1/3 CUP	GRATED PARMESAN CHEESE	75 ML
1/4 CUP	FINELY CHOPPED FRESH PARSLEY	60 ML
I	LARGE EGG, LIGHTLY BEATEN	I
I TSP	GRATED LEMON ZEST	5 ML
I TSP	GARLIC POWDER	5 ML
1/2 TSP	EACH SALT AND BLACK PEPPER	2 ML
2 TBSP	CANOLA OIL	30 ML

IN A MEDIUM BOWL, MIX TURKEY, ZUCCHINI, BREAD CRUMBS, PARMESAN, PARSLEY, EGG, LEMON ZEST, GARLIC POWDER, SALT AND PEPPER UNTIL WELL COMBINED. USING A SMALL ICE CREAM SCOOP OR 2-TBSP (30 ML) MEASURE, SCOOP AND ROLL MIXTURE INTO MEATBALLS. IN A LARGE NONSTICK SKILLET, OVER MEDIUM HEAT, HEAT OIL. ADD MEATBALLS AND COOK, TURNING OCCASIONALLY, ABOUT 15 MINUTES OR UNTIL GOLDEN AND COOKED THROUGH. MAKES ABOUT 26 MEATBALLS. SERVES 4.

MAKE AHEAD: STORE COOKED MEATBALLS IN A FREEZER-SAFE CONTAINER FOR UP TO 2 MONTHS.

TIP: THE MEATBALLS CAN ALSO BE BAKED IN THE OVEN. PREHEAT OVEN TO 350°F (180°C) AND SET ASIDE A PARCHMENT PAPER LINED OR LIGHTLY GREASED BAKING SHEET. PLACE MEATBALLS ON PREPARED BAKING SHEET AND BAKE 25 TO 30 MINUTES, OR UNTIL COOKED THROUGH. (OMIT THE 2 TBSP/15 ML OIL FOR THIS VERSION.)

CHICKEN PICCATA AND PEAS

THIS IS A TANGY CLASSIC ITALIAN DISH USING CHICKEN CUTLETS. SO QUICK AND EASY, IT'S SOMETHING YOU MAY FIND YOURSELF MAKING EVERY WEEK.

I LB	THIN CHICKEN CUTLETS OR CHICKEN BREAST SLICES	500 G
1/4 TSP	SALT	I ML
PINCH	BLACK PEPPER	PINCH
1/4 CUP	ALL-PURPOSE FLOUR	60 ML
3 TBSP	BUTTER, DIVIDED	45 ML
2 TBSP	CANOLA OIL	30 ML
I CUP	READY-TO-USE CHICKEN BROTH	250 ML
I CUP	FROZEN OR FRESH PEAS	250 ML
1/2 TSP	GRATED LEMON ZEST	2 ML
I TBSP	LEMON JUICE	15 ML
2 TBSP	CHOPPED FRESH ITALIAN PARSLEY	30 ML

SPRINKLE CHICKEN WITH SALT AND PEPPER. DREDGE CUTLETS IN FLOUR TO COAT AND SHAKE OFF ANY EXCESS.

IN NONSTICK SKILLET, MELT 2 TBSP (30 ML) OF THE BUTTER AND THE OIL OVER MEDIUM-HIGH HEAT AND COOK CUTLETS, IN BATCHES IF NECESSARY, FOR ABOUT 8 MINUTES OR UNTIL GOLDEN, TURNING ONCE. REMOVE TO PLATTER AND KEEP WARM.

ADD BROTH AND PEAS TO SKILLET AND BRING TO BOIL. BOIL FOR ABOUT 3 MINUTES OR UNTIL REDUCED BY HALF, SCRAPING UP BROWN BITS. ADD LEMON ZEST AND JUICE, PARSLEY AND REMAINING BUTTER AND STIR UNTIL

BUTTER IS MELTED. RETURN CHICKEN TO PAN TO HEAT THROUGH AND SIMMER FOR ABOUT 2 MINUTES OR UNTIL CHICKEN IS NO LONGER PINK INSIDE. SERVES 4

TIP: THIS RECIPE IS EASY TO DOUBLE FOR A LARGER CROWD.

TIP: IF YOU CAN'T FIND CHICKEN CUTLETS, MAKE YOUR OWN BY SIMPLY CUTTING BONELESS SKINLESS CHICKEN BREAST IN HALF HORIZONTALLY TO MAKE A THIN, EVEN CUTLET.

I ORDERED A CHICKEN AND AN EGG
FROM AMAZON. I'LL LET YOU KNOW.

BALSAMIC CHICKEN AND MUSHROOMS

THIS DELICIOUS SKILLET MEAL TURNS BASIC
CHICKEN INTO A FLAVORFUL FAVORITE. SERVE WITH
PASTA, RICE OR MASHED POTATOES TO SOP UP
ALL THE SCRUMPTIOUS RICH GRAVY.

3 TSP	CANOLA OIL, DIVIDED	15 ML
8	BONELESS, SKINLESS CHICKEN THIGHS	8
1/2 TSP	EACH SALT AND BLACK PEPPER	2 ML
I LB	CREMINI MUSHROOMS, SLICED	500 G
3 TBSP	BALSAMIC VINEGAR	45 ML
I TBSP	SOY SAUCE	15 ML
4	GARLIC CLOVES, MINCED	4
1/2 TSP	DRIED THYME	2 ML
1/2 CUP	HEAVY OR WHIPPING (35%) CREAM	125 ML
2 TSP	CORNSTARCH	10 ML
1/2 CUP	CHOPPED FRESH PARSLEY	125 ML

IN A LARGE SKILLET, OVER MEDIUM-HIGH HEAT, HEAT
I TSP (5 ML) OIL; ADD CHICKEN THIGHS, PLACING THEM IN
A SINGLE LAYER; SPRINKLE WITH SALT AND PEPPER. COOK
FOR 6 MINUTES, THEN TURN CHICKEN OVER AND COOK
ANOTHER 6 MINUTES. TRANSFER CHICKEN TO A PLATE
AND KEEP WARM.

IN SAME SKILLET, WITHOUT CLEANING, ADD REMAINING
2 TSP (IO ML) OIL AND MUSHROOMS; COOK, STIRRING
OCCASIONALLY, FOR 8 MINUTES, UNTIL MUSHROOMS
BEGIN TO BROWN. REDUCE HEAT TO MEDIUM AND

ADD VINEGAR, SOY SAUCE, GARLIC AND THYME; COOK
3 MINUTES, STIRRING OCCASIONALLY. IN A SMALL BOWL,
WHISK TOGETHER CREAM AND CORNSTARCH, THEN STIR
INTO MUSHROOM MIXTURE. RETURN CHICKEN AND ANY
ACCUMULATED JUICES TO THE PAN. COVER AND COOK
5 MINUTES, OR UNTIL CHICKEN IS COOKED THROUGH.
SPRINKLE WITH PARSLEY. SERVES 4 TO 6.

TIP: LEFTOVERS CAN BE REFRIGERATED AND STORED IN AN
AIRTIGHT CONTAINER FOR UP TO 4 DAYS.

SKILLET CHICKEN AND COUSCOUS

THIS ONE-PAN MEAL IS FULL OF FLAVOR AND WILL MAKE YOUR HOUSE SMELL DELICIOUS! ANY LEFTOVERS WOULD MAKE A TASTY FILLING FOR A TORTILLA WRAP. IF YOU LIKE YOUR MEAL EXTRA ZESTY, SERVED WITH LEMON WEDGES.

3 TBSP	CANOLA OIL, DIVIDED	45 ML
I LB	BONELESS, SKINLESS CHICKEN THIGHS, CUT INTO I-INCH (2.5 CM) CUBES	500 G
½ TSP	EACH SALT AND BLACK PEPPER	2 ML
1¾ CUPS	READY-TO-USE CHICKEN BROTH	425 ML
2 TBSP	LEMON JUICE	30 ML
2 TSP	DRIED OREGANO	10 ML
I TSP	GARLIC POWDER	5 ML
I TSP	ONION POWDER	5 ML
1½ CUPS	INSTANT COUSCOUS	375 ML
I CUP	CRUMBLED FETA CHEESE (ABOUT 4 OZ/125 G)	250 ML
¼ CUP	CHOPPED FRESH DILL	60 ML
I TSP	GRATED LEMON ZEST	5 ML

IN A LARGE NONSTICK SKILLET, OVER MEDIUM-HIGH HEAT, HEAT I TBSP (15 ML) OIL; ADD CHICKEN, SPRINKLE WITH SALT AND PEPPER. COOK, STIRRING OCCASIONALLY UNTIL GOLDEN BROWN, ABOUT 7 MINUTES OR UNTIL COOKED THROUGH. REMOVE CHICKEN TO A PLATE. IN THE SAME SKILLET, WITHOUT CLEANING, REDUCE HEAT TO MEDIUM AND ADD BROTH, REMAINING 2 TBSP (30 ML) OIL, LEMON

JUICE, OREGANO, GARLIC POWDER AND ONION POWDER AND BRING TO SIMMER, SCRAPING UP ANY BROWN BITS FROM THE BOTTOM OF THE SKILLET. STIR IN COUSCOUS. RETURN CHICKEN AND ANY ACCUMULATED JUICES TO PAN AND NESTLE PIECES INTO COUSCOUS.

COVER, REMOVE FROM HEAT AND ALLOW TO REST 5 MINUTES, UNTIL ALL THE LIQUID IS ABSORBED AND COUSCOUS IS TENDER. (IF THE COUSCOUS STILL IS A LITTLE CRUNCHY, LET SIT FOR FEW MORE MINUTES.) STIR IN FETA, DILL AND LEMON ZEST JUST BEFORE SERVING. SERVES 4 TO 5.

TIP: ZEST YOUR LEMON BEFORE JUICING.

TIP: YOU CAN SUBSTITUTE 4 TSP (20 ML) OF DRIED DILL FOR THE $1/4$ CUP (60 ML) FRESH DILL.

CHICKEN CASSOULET

THIS IS A FABULOUS MEAL TO SHARE WITH YOUR FAMILY ON A COOL FALL OR WINTER EVENING. USING BONELESS CHICKEN THIGHS MAKES IT EASY TO SERVE UP AND REDUCES THE TRADITIONAL LONG COOKING TIME.

CASSOULET

4	SLICES BACON, CHOPPED	4
2 TBSP	CANOLA OIL, DIVIDED	30 ML
1½ LB	BONELESS SKINLESS CHICKEN THIGHS	750 G
3	GARLIC CLOVES, MINCED	3
2	CARROTS, SLICED	2
1	ONION, CHOPPED	1
1	CELERY STALK, CHOPPED	1
1	CAN (19 OZ/540 ML) PETITE CUT TOMATOES (SEE TIP)	1
1	BAY LEAF	1
½ TSP	DRIED ROSEMARY	2 ML
½ TSP	DRIED THYME	2 ML
¼ TSP	EACH SALT AND BLACK PEPPER	1 ML
1	CAN (19 OZ/540 ML) WHITE KIDNEY BEANS, RINSED AND DRAINED	1

TOPPING

1 CUP	FRESH BREAD CRUMBS	250 ML
2 TBSP	CHOPPED FRESH PARSLEY	30 ML
¼ CUP	GRATED PARMESAN CHEESE	60 ML
2 TBSP	BUTTER, MELTED	30 ML

CASSOULET: IN A LARGE OVENPROOF DUTCH OVEN, COOK BACON OVER MEDIUM-HIGH HEAT UNTIL CRISP. REMOVE

WITH SLOTTED SPOON TO A PAPER TOWEL LINED PLATE; SET ASIDE. ADD 1 TBSP (15 ML) OF THE OIL AND RETURN POT TO MEDIUM-HIGH HEAT. BROWN CHICKEN ALL OVER, IN BATCHES IF NECESSARY; REMOVE TO ANOTHER PLATE.

REDUCE HEAT TO MEDIUM; ADD REMAINING OIL AND COOK GARLIC, CARROTS, ONION AND CELERY, STIRRING, FOR ABOUT 5 MINUTES OR UNTIL SOFTENED. ADD TOMATOES, BAY LEAF, ROSEMARY, THYME, SALT AND PEPPER, STIRRING TO SCRAPE UP BROWN BITS. BRING TO A BOIL.

ADD BEANS, COOKED BACON AND BROWNED CHICKEN TO VEGETABLES; RETURN TO A SIMMER. COVER AND SIMMER FOR ABOUT 20 MINUTES OR UNTIL JUICES RUN CLEAR WHEN CHICKEN IS PIERCED. DISCARD BAY LEAF.

MAKE-AHEAD: COOL IN REFRIGERATOR AND THEN COVER AND REFRIGERATE FOR UP TO 1 DAY OR STORE IN AIRTIGHT CONTAINER AND FREEZE FOR UP TO 2 MONTHS.

TOPPING: IN A BOWL, COMBINE BREAD CRUMBS, PARSLEY, CHEESE AND BUTTER; SPRINKLE OVER CASSOULET. BROIL ABOUT 6 INCHES (15 CM) BELOW THE BROILER ELEMENT FOR ABOUT 1 MINUTE OR UNTIL BREAD CRUMBS ARE GOLDEN BROWN. SERVES 6.

TIP: IF NOT SERVING CASSOULET IMMEDIATELY, YOU CAN REHEAT WITH TOPPING IN 350°F (180°C) OVEN FOR ABOUT 30 MINUTES OR UNTIL BUBBLY AND HEATED THROUGH. IF FROZEN, THAW IN REFRIGERATOR, THEN SPRINKLE WITH TOPPING BEFORE BAKING AND ADD ADDITIONAL COOKING TIME TO HEAT THROUGH.

TIP: TO MAKE FRESH BREAD CRUMBS, USE FRESH SLICED BREAD OR BUNS AND PULSE IN A FOOD PROCESSOR UNTIL BROKEN INTO SMALL CRUMBS. MEASURE WHAT YOU NEED AND FREEZE THE REST; YOU WILL HAVE FRESH BREAD CRUMBS AT THE READY FOR NEXT TIME.

TIP: PETITE CUT TOMATOES ARE SMALLER DICED CANNED TOMATOES THAT ARE USUALLY STEWED AND HAVE ADDITIONAL FLAVORS ADDED; YOU CAN USE THE ORIGINAL STEWED IN THIS RECIPE OR LOOK FOR GARLIC AND OLIVE OIL.

SMOKED PAPRIKA GARLIC CHICKEN

THIS FLAVORFUL CHICKEN IS A LITTLE SWEET WITH A TOUCH OF HEAT! SERVE WITH POTATOES OR A RICE SIDE DISH.

3 TBSP	CIDER VINEGAR	45 ML
1½ TBSP	SMOKED PAPRIKA	22 ML
1 TBSP	CANOLA OIL	15 ML
1 TBSP	LIQUID HONEY	15 ML
2 TSP	GARLIC POWDER	10 ML
1 TSP	EACH SALT AND BLACK PEPPER	5 ML
10	BONE-IN, SKIN-ON CHICKEN THIGHS OR DRUMSTICKS	10

IN A SHALLOW BAKING DISH OR RESEALABLE PLASTIC BAG, MIX TOGETHER VINEGAR, PAPRIKA, OIL, HONEY, GARLIC POWDER, SALT AND PEPPER. ADD CHICKEN PIECES AND MIX TO EVENLY COAT. COVER AND REFRIGERATE FOR AT LEAST 4 HOURS OR UP TO 24 HOURS, TURNING ONCE OR TWICE.

PREHEAT OVEN TO 425°F (220°C). LINE A LARGE RIMMED BAKING SHEET WITH FOIL AND PLACE A WIRE RACK ON TOP; SPRAY RACK WITH NONSTICK COOKING SPRAY. ARRANGE MARINATED CHICKEN PIECES IN A SINGLE LAYER ON RACK; DRIZZLE ANY REMAINING MARINADE OVER TOP. BAKE 35 MINUTES OR UNTIL CHICKEN IS NO LONGER PINK IN THE MIDDLE. TURN ON THE BROILER AND MOVE OVEN RACK TO 6 INCHES (15 CM) BELOW THE BROILER ELEMENT. BROIL ABOUT 1 TO 2 MINUTES UNTIL LIGHTLY GOLDEN AND CHICKEN REGISTERS 165°F (74°C). SERVES 6 TO 8.

PENNE FRITTATA WITH SMOKED CHICKEN

SMOKED CHICKEN IS READILY AVAILABLE IN THE DELI SECTION OF THE GROCERY STORE OR YOUR FAVORITE DELI SHOP. SERVE THIS DISH WITH A SALAD ON THE SIDE.

8 OZ	DRIED PENNE PASTA (ABOUT 3 CUPS/750 ML)	250 G
8	LARGE EGGS	8
2 TSP	DRIED ITALIAN SEASONING	10 ML
1/2 TSP	BLACK PEPPER	2 ML
2 CUPS	CHOPPED SMOKED CHICKEN	500 ML
1 CUP	FROZEN PEAS, THAWED	250 ML
1/2 CUP	GRATED PARMESAN CHEESE	125 ML
1/2 CUP	SHREDDED MOZZARELLA CHEESE	125 ML
2 TBSP	CANOLA OIL	30 ML

IN A LARGE POT OF BOILING SALTED WATER, COOK PENNE FOR ABOUT 10 MINUTES OR UNTIL AL DENTE. DRAIN WELL AND SET ASIDE. IN A LARGE BOWL, WHISK TOGETHER EGGS, ITALIAN SEASONING AND PEPPER. ADD PENNE, CHICKEN, PEAS, PARMESAN AND MOZZARELLA, STIRRING GENTLY TO COMBINE.

IN A LARGE NONSTICK SKILLET, HEAT OIL OVER MEDIUM HEAT. POUR IN PENNE MIXTURE AND SMOOTH TOP. COOK FOR ABOUT 10 MINUTES, JIGGLING THE PAN TO MAKE SURE IT DOESN'T STICK, UNTIL ALMOST SET. PLACE A LARGE PLATE OVER THE PAN AND INVERT FRITTATA

ONTO PLATE. SLIDE FRITTATA BACK INTO PAN AND COOK FOR ABOUT 10 MINUTES OR UNTIL THE CENTER IS SET AND NO LIQUID APPEARS WHEN FRITTATA IS PIERCED WITH A FORK. SERVES 6.

TIP: SUBSTITUTE THE PEAS WITH 1 CUP (250 ML) COOKED AND CHOPPED LEFTOVER VEGETABLES.

TIP: IF YOU DO NOT HAVE A LARGE SKILLET, DIVIDE AND COOK THE PASTA MIXTURE IN TWO SMALLER SKILLETS.

WHAT DO YOU CALL AN ACADEMICALLY
SUCCESSFUL SLICE OF BREAD?
AN HONOR ROLL.

SPICED CHICKPEA CHICKEN AND RICE

WE LOVE THE SHORTCUT OF USING GROCERY-STORE
ROTISSERIE CHICKEN AND FROZEN VEGETABLES TO
SPEED UP MEAL PREPARATION. YOU CAN GARNISH
THIS AROMATIC DISH WITH TOASTED NUTS, SUCH AS
ALMONDS, PISTACHIOS OR CASHEWS, IF DESIRED.

3 TBSP	CANOLA OIL	45 ML
I	ONION, CHOPPED	I
1 1/3 CUPS	UNCOOKED LONG-GRAIN WHITE RICE (SUCH AS BASMATI OR JASMINE)	325 ML
I	CAN (19 OZ/540 ML) CHICKPEAS, RINSED AND DRAINED	I
I TSP	GROUND CINNAMON	5 ML
I TSP	SALT	5 ML
1/2 TSP	BLACK PEPPER	2 ML
1/2 TSP	GROUND CARDAMOM	2 ML
1/2 TSP	GROUND TURMERIC	2 ML
1/4 TSP	GROUND CLOVES	I ML
2 CUPS	READY-TO-USE CHICKEN BROTH	500 ML
2 CUPS	COOKED CUBED CHICKEN	500 ML
2 CUPS	FROZEN MIXED PEAS AND CARROTS, THAWED	500 ML

IN A LARGE SKILLET, OVER MEDIUM-HIGH HEAT, HEAT
OIL; ADD ONION AND COOK, STIRRING OCCASIONALLY, FOR
5 MINUTES, UNTIL ONION BEGINS TO SOFTEN. STIR IN
RICE, CHICKPEAS, CINNAMON, SALT, PEPPER, CARDAMOM,
TURMERIC AND CLOVES; COOK 30 SECONDS, THEN STIR

IN BROTH. BRING TO A SIMMER, COVER AND REDUCE HEAT TO MEDIUM-LOW; COOK 25 MINUTES. STIR IN CHICKEN AND MIXED VEGETABLES. COVER AND COOK ANOTHER 5 MINUTES, OR UNTIL HEATED THROUGH. SERVES 6.

TIP: TO SPEED UP THE COOKING PROCESS, MEASURE RICE AND SPICES AHEAD OF TIME. THE ONION CAN BE CHOPPED, COVERED AND REFRIGERATED UNTIL READY TO USE.

SWEET GARLIC CHICKEN

THIS BAKED CHICKEN IS SWEET, GARLICKY AND MOUTH-WATERING! THE LONGER THE CHICKEN IS MARINATED, THE MORE FLAVORFUL IT WILL BE.

1/4 CUP	PACKED DARK BROWN SUGAR	60 ML
6	GARLIC CLOVES, MINCED	6
3 TBSP	FISH SAUCE	45 ML
2 TBSP	FRESH LIME JUICE	30 ML
1 TBSP	GROUND TURMERIC	15 ML
1 TSP	ONION POWDER	5 ML
1 TSP	BLACK PEPPER	5 ML
1 TSP	SRIRACHA	5 ML
10	BONE-IN, SKIN-ON CHICKEN THIGHS	10
	LIME WEDGES	

IN A SHALLOW BAKING DISH, MIX TOGETHER BROWN SUGAR, GARLIC, FISH SAUCE, LIME JUICE, TURMERIC, ONION POWDER, PEPPER AND SRIRACHA. ADD CHICKEN PIECES AND MIX TO COAT EVENLY. (YOU CAN ALSO MIX THE MARINADE IN A RESEALABLE BAG FOR EASIER CLEANUP.) COVER AND REFRIGERATE FOR AT LEAST 4 HOURS OR UP TO 24 HOURS.

PREHEAT OVEN TO 425°F (220°C). LINE A LARGE RIMMED BAKING SHEET WITH FOIL AND PLACE A WIRE RACK ON TOP; SPRAY RACK WITH NONSTICK COOKING SPRAY. ARRANGE CHICKEN PIECES IN A SINGLE LAYER ON RACK, DRIZZLE ANY REMAINING MARINADE OVER TOP. BAKE 35 MINUTES OR UNTIL CHICKEN IS NO LONGER PINK IN THE MIDDLE.

TURN ON THE BROILER AND MOVE OVEN RACK TO 6 INCHES (15 CM) BELOW THE BROILER ELEMENT. BROIL 1 TO 2 MINUTES UNTIL LIGHTLY GOLDEN AND CHICKEN REGISTERS 165°F (74°C). SERVE WITH LIME WEDGES ON THE SIDE. SERVES 6 TO 8.

TIP: TURN ANY CHICKEN LEFTOVERS INTO A TASTY SANDWICH FILLING. REMOVE THE BONES, SHRED CHICKEN AND ADD GRATED CARROT, CILANTRO, LETTUCE, MAYONNAISE AND A DRIZZLE OF SRIRACHA.

GERMANY IS NOW ADVISING PEOPLE
TO STOCK UP ON CHEESE AND SAUSAGES.
THIS IS CALLED THE WURST KÄSE SCENARIO.

TURKEY NUGGETS

LITTLE BITES OF TURKEY ARE PERFECT
FOR LITTLE HANDS TO GRAB AND DIP INTO
THEIR FAVORITE SAUCE. WHEN THESE ARE SERVED
ALONGSIDE SOME OVEN FRIES, YOU KNOW YOUR
KIDS WILL GOBBLE UP THEIR DINNER!

1	BONELESS SKINLESS TURKEY BREAST, ABOUT (1 LB/500 G)	1
1 TBSP	CANOLA OIL	15 ML
1 TSP	CHILI POWDER	5 ML
1/2 TSP	GARLIC POWDER	2 ML
1/2 TSP	EACH SALT AND BLACK PEPPER	2 ML
2 TBSP	ALL-PURPOSE FLOUR	30 ML
1	LARGE EGG	1
2 1/2 CUPS	CORN FLAKES CEREAL, CRUSHED	625 ML
1 TBSP	MINCED FRESH PARSLEY (OPTIONAL)	15 ML
	HONEY MUSTARD, BARBECUE SAUCE OR KETCHUP	

CUT TURKEY INTO ABOUT TWENTY 1 1/2-INCH (4 CM)
CHUNKS AND PLACE IN A BOWL. ADD OIL, CHILI POWDER,
GARLIC POWDER, SALT AND PEPPER; TOSS TO COAT
EVENLY. SPRINKLE FLOUR OVER TOP AND TOSS TO
COAT WELL.

PREHEAT OVEN TO 400°F (200°C). LINE A BAKING SHEET
WITH PARCHMENT PAPER. PLACE EGG IN A SHALLOW BOWL
AND BEAT LIGHTLY WITH A FORK. IN ANOTHER SHALLOW
DISH, COMBINE CORN FLAKES AND PARSLEY. DIP A FEW

PIECES OF TURKEY AT A TIME INTO EGG AND REMOVE, LETTING EXCESS DRIP OFF. PLACE IN CORN FLAKES MIXTURE AND COAT WELL. PLACE ON PREPARED BAKING SHEET. REPEAT WITH REMAINING TURKEY PIECES.

BAKE FOR ABOUT 15 MINUTES, UNTIL GOLDEN AND NO LONGER PINK INSIDE, TURNING HALFWAY THROUGH. SERVE WITH YOUR FAVORITE SAUCES. SERVES 4.

I ALWAYS KNOCK ON THE FRIDGE
BEFORE I OPEN IT. JUST IN CASE
THERE'S A SALAD DRESSING.

TURKEY PASTA TETRAZZINI

*TURKEY TOSSED WITH PASTA MAKES
AN EASY WEEKNIGHT CLASSIC.*

3 CUPS	DRIED CAVATAPPI OR ROTINI PASTA	750 ML
3 TBSP	BUTTER	45 ML
I LB	BONELESS SKINLESS TURKEY BREAST, CUBED	500 G
1/2 TSP	EACH SALT AND BLACK PEPPER	2 ML
8 OZ	SLICED MUSHROOMS	250 G
2	GARLIC CLOVES, MINCED	2
2 TBSP	ALL-PURPOSE FLOUR	30 ML
2 CUPS	MILK	500 ML
I CUP	FROZEN OR FRESH PEAS	250 ML
1/2 CUP	GRATED PARMESAN CHEESE	125 ML

IN A POT OF BOILING SALTED WATER, COOK PASTA FOR ABOUT 8 MINUTES OR UNTIL AL DENTE. DRAIN WELL AND SET ASIDE.

MEANWHILE, IN A LARGE SKILLET, MELT BUTTER OVER MEDIUM-HIGH HEAT. BROWN TURKEY WITH SALT AND PEPPER ON BOTH SIDES. ADD MUSHROOMS AND GARLIC AND COOK, STIRRING, FOR 6 MINUTES OR UNTIL MUSHROOMS ARE STARTING TO BROWN. STIR IN FLOUR AND COOK I MINUTE. ADD MILK AND BRING TO A BOIL, STIRRING CONSTANTLY. ADD PEAS; REDUCE HEAT AND SIMMER, STIRRING OCCASIONALLY, FOR ABOUT 5 MINUTES OR UNTIL STARTING TO THICKEN. STIR IN CHEESE AND COOKED PASTA AND TOSS TO COAT WELL. SERVES 4.

Buffalo Chicken Chowder (page 88)

Sausage Potato Soup with Greens (page 90)

Cheeseburger Pie (page 97)

**Sun-Dried Tomato Oil and Herb Grilled Steak (page 103)
with Roasted Veggie Pan (page 208)**

**Soy Lime Beef and Pepper Skewers (page 104)
with Spanish Rice (page 196)**

Lemongrass Chicken with Noodles (page 106)

Turkey Zucchini Meatballs (page 108)

Skillet Chicken and Couscous (page 114)

PORK AND LAMB

SPIRAL PASTA TACO SKILLET SUPPER

ADDING YOUR PASTA RIGHT INTO THIS SKILLET SUPPER MAKES IT EASY TO GET DINNER ON THE TABLE. SERVE IT UP WITH YOUR FAVORITE TACO TOPPINGS!

I TBSP	CANOLA OIL	15 ML
I	ONION, FINELY CHOPPED	I
2	GARLIC CLOVES, MINCED	2
I LB	LEAN GROUND PORK	500 G
2 TSP	CHILI POWDER	10 ML
2 TSP	DRIED OREGANO	10 ML
I TSP	GROUND CUMIN	5 ML
1/4 TSP	HOT PEPPER FLAKES	I ML
1/4 TSP	SALT	I ML
2 1/2 CUPS	WATER	625 ML
2 CUPS	MEDIUM SALSA	500 ML
2 CUPS	DRIED ROTINI OR FUSILLI PASTA	500 ML
I	GREEN OR YELLOW BELL PEPPER, CHOPPED	I
1/2 CUP	SHREDDED TEX-MEX CHEESE BLEND	250 ML
	CHOPPED FRESH CILANTRO (OPTIONAL)	
	SOUR CREAM (OPTIONAL)	

IN A NONSTICK SKILLET, HEAT OIL OVER MEDIUM HEAT. COOK ONION AND GARLIC FOR 3 MINUTES OR UNTIL SOFTENED. ADD PORK, CHILI POWDER, OREGANO, CUMIN, HOT PEPPER FLAKES AND SALT. COOK, STIRRING, FOR

5 MINUTES OR UNTIL BROWNED. STIR IN WATER, SALSA AND ROTINI AND GREEN PEPPER; STIR TO COMBINE. BRING TO A GENTLE SIMMER; COOK, STIRRING OCCASIONALLY FOR ABOUT 15 MINUTES OR UNTIL PASTA IS AL DENTE AND SAUCE IS THICKENED. STIR IN CHEESE BEFORE SERVING. TOP WITH CILANTRO AND SOUR CREAM IF DESIRED. SERVES 4.

PASTA LA VISTA, BABY.

SKILLET EGG ROLL WITH WONTON CRISPS

TAKE ALL THE INGREDIENTS IN AN EGG ROLL
AND CREATE THIS EASY ONE-SKILLET MEAL. YOU
WON'T MISS THE CRUNCH OF THE EGG ROLL WRAPPER
WHEN YOU SERVE THE EGG ROLL MIXTURE ON
TOP OF THE WONTON CRISPS.

WONTON CRISPS

24	WONTON WRAPPERS	24
	SESAME OR CANOLA OIL	

SKILLET EGG ROLL

1 TBSP	SESAME OIL	15 ML
1 LB	LEAN GROUND PORK	500 G
1 TBSP	MINCED FRESH GINGER	15 ML
2	GARLIC CLOVES, MINCED	2
1/4 TSP	EACH SALT AND BLACK PEPPER	1 ML
3 CUPS	COLESLAW MIX	750 ML
2	GREEN ONIONS, THINLY SLICED	2
3 TBSP	SOY SAUCE	45 ML
2 CUPS	FRESH BEAN SPROUTS (OPTIONAL)	500 ML

PREHEAT OVEN TO 400°F (200°C). SET ASIDE A LARGE
BAKING SHEET.

WONTON CRISPS: BRUSH WONTON WRAPPERS WITH
SESAME OR CANOLA OIL AND PLACE HALF ON BAKING
SHEET. BAKE FOR ABOUT 4 MINUTES OR UNTIL GOLDEN
BROWN. REPEAT WITH REMAINING WRAPPERS. LET COOL.

SKILLET EGG ROLL: IN A LARGE NONSTICK SKILLET, HEAT OIL OVER MEDIUM-HIGH HEAT. ADD PORK, GINGER, GARLIC, SALT AND PEPPER; COOK, STIRRING FOR ABOUT 4 MINUTES OR UNTIL PORK IS NO LONGER PINK. STIR IN COLESLAW MIX, GREEN ONIONS AND SOY SAUCE; COOK, STIRRING FOR ABOUT 3 MINUTES OR UNTIL COLESLAW IS WILTED. STIR IN BEAN SPROUTS, IF USING, AND TOSS TO COMBINE. SERVE ON TOP OF WONTON CRISPS. SERVES 4.

ORANGE HOISIN BROCCOLI AND PORK

THIS FLAVOR COMBINATION ALWAYS SEEMS TO BE A DINNERTIME FAVORITE THE WHOLE FAMILY CAN AGREE ON.

1	BUNCH BROCCOLI	1
2 TBSP	CANOLA OIL, DIVIDED	30 ML
1 LB	LEAN GROUND PORK	500 G
1 TBSP	MINCED FRESH GINGER	15 ML
2	GARLIC CLOVES, MINCED	2
2	GREEN ONIONS, THINLY SLICED	2
1/3 CUP	ORANGE JUICE OR READY-TO-USE CHICKEN BROTH	75 ML
1/3 CUP	HOISIN SAUCE	75 ML
2 TBSP	SOY SAUCE	30 ML
1 TSP	CORNSTARCH	5 ML

CUT BROCCOLI INTO BITE-SIZE FLORETS AND PEEL STEMS. CUT STEM INTO BITE-SIZE PIECES AS WELL.

IN A LARGE SKILLET, HEAT 1 TBSP (15 ML) OF THE OIL OVER MEDIUM-HIGH HEAT. ADD BROCCOLI AND STIR-FRY FOR 4 MINUTES OR UNTIL STARTING TO TURN BRIGHT GREEN. REMOVE TO A BOWL. RETURN SKILLET TO MEDIUM-HIGH HEAT AND ADD REMAINING OIL. ADD PORK, GINGER, GARLIC AND GREEN ONIONS AND COOK, STIRRING, FOR ABOUT 4 MINUTES OR UNTIL NO LONGER PINK.

MEANWHILE IN A BOWL, WHISK TOGETHER ORANGE JUICE, HOISIN, SOY SAUCE AND CORNSTARCH. POUR INTO SKILLET AND RETURN BROCCOLI TO SKILLET. COOK, STIRRING, FOR ABOUT 2 MINUTES OR UNTIL WELL COATED AND THICKENED. SERVES 4.

TIP: IF LOOKING FOR A BLAST OF HEAT, SIMPLY DRIZZLE SRIRACHA OVER TOP OR ADD A PINCH OF HOT PEPPER FLAKES WHEN COOKING THE PORK MIXTURE.

TIP: EMILY'S FRIEND RANI LOVES TO SERVE THIS WITH RAMEN NOODLES RIGHT IN THE SKILLET. SIMPLY COOK THE NOODLES FOR ABOUT 2 MINUTES, DRAIN AND ADD TO THE SKILLET WITH THE PORK AND BROCCOLI TO TOSS TOGETHER AND SERVE.

ADRIANA'S PIZZA TACOS

WHEN SHE IS HUNGRY, EMILY'S TEENAGE DAUGHTER ADRIANA WILL MAKE SURE SHE HAS THESE SIMPLE INGREDIENTS TO WHIP UP A COUPLE OF THESE EASY TACOS. (DON'T TELL HER, BUT THEY'RE REALLY QUESADILLAS.)

2	SMALL WHOLE WHEAT FLOUR TORTILLAS	2
2 TBSP	PIZZA SAUCE	30 ML
1/3 CUP	SHREDDED MOZZARELLA CHEESE	75 ML
8	SLICES PEPPERONI (ABOUT 2 INCHES/2.5 CM ROUND)	8

PREHEAT OVEN TO 350°F (180°C). SET ASIDE A LARGE BAKING SHEET.

PLACE TORTILLAS ON BAKING SHEET. SPREAD PIZZA SAUCE OVER BOTH. SPRINKLE EACH WITH CHEESE AND TOP WITH PEPPERONI. BAKE FOR ABOUT 8 MINUTES OR UNTIL CHEESE IS MELTED AND TORTILLA EDGES ARE GOLDEN. REMOVE FROM OVEN AND USING TONGS, FOLD EACH TORTILLA IN HALF AND PRESS GENTLY. LET COOL SLIGHTLY BEFORE TAKING SOME BIG BITES. SERVES 1.

GLAZED PEAMEAL BACON ROAST

ENJOY THIS EASY ROAST FOR BREAKFAST, BRUNCH OR DINNER! THE ZIP OF MUSTARD AND PEPPER IN THE PAN SAUCE MAKES IT PERFECT FOR DRIZZLING OVER THE SLICES WHEN SERVING.

I	WHOLE PEAMEAL BACON ROAST (ABOUT 2 LB/I KG)	I
1/2 CUP	ORANGE JUICE	125 ML
1/3 CUP	MAPLE SYRUP	75 ML
I TBSP	GRAINY OR DIJON MUSTARD	15 ML
1/4 TSP	BLACK PEPPER	I ML

PLACE ROAST IN A SHALLOW BAKING DISH, FAT SIDE UP. USING A SHARP KNIFE, MAKE LONG CUTS ACROSS THE TOP INTO THE FAT BUT NOT TOO FAR INTO THE MEAT. REPEAT CROSSWISE TO CREATE A DIAMOND PATTERN ON THE ROAST. PREHEAT OVEN TO 375°F (190°C).

IN A BOWL, WHISK TOGETHER ORANGE JUICE, MAPLE SYRUP, MUSTARD AND PEPPER. SPOON ABOUT HALF OF THE MIXTURE OVER TOP OF ROAST. COVER WITH FOIL AND ROAST FOR 45 MINUTES. UNCOVER AND SPOON REMAINING ORANGE JUICE MIXTURE OVER TOP AND RETURN TO OVEN FOR ABOUT 30 MINUTES OR UNTIL WELL GLAZED AND MEAT THERMOMETER REACHES 130°F (55°C).

LET STAND ABOUT 10 MINUTES BEFORE PLACING ON CUTTING BOARD AND SLICE THINLY. SERVE WITH PAN SAUCE. SERVES 6 TO 8.

A BOWL OF FLAVORFUL FRIED RICE TOPPED WITH A FRIED EGG IS A DELICIOUS COMFORT FOOD. KIMCHI IS KOREAN SALTED AND FERMENTED CABBAGE AND RADISH STAPLE THAT ADDS A DELICIOUS TANG AND FLAVOR TO THE FRIED RICE. IT'S USUALLY FOUND IN THE REFRIGERATED INTERNATIONAL FOOD SECTION OF MOST GROCERY STORES. BE SURE TO SERVE SRIRACHA SAUCE ON THE SIDE FOR EXTRA FLAVOR AND HEAT.

RICE

8	SLICES BACON, CHOPPED INTO $1/4$-INCH (0.5 CM) PIECES	8
1½ CUPS	KIMCHI, CHOPPED	375 ML
6 CUPS	LEFTOVER COOKED RICE	1.5 L
1 TBSP	SESAME OIL	15 ML
1 TBSP	SOY SAUCE	15 ML
1 TSP	GARLIC POWDER	5 ML
3	GREEN ONIONS, SLICED	3
1 TBSP	ROASTED SESAME SEEDS	15 ML

EGGS

2 TSP	CANOLA OIL	10 ML
4	LARGE EGGS	4

IN A LARGE NONSTICK SKILLET, OVER MEDIUM HEAT, COOK BACON ABOUT 8 MINUTES OR UNTIL LIGHTLY CRISP. USING A SLOTTED SPOON, TRANSFER BACON TO A PLATE; SET ASIDE. REMOVE ALL BUT 2 TBSP (30 ML) BACON FAT. IN THE SAME SKILLET, OVER MEDIUM-HIGH HEAT, ADD KIMCHI,

INCLUDING ANY OF THE JUICE, AND FRY ABOUT 4 MINUTES OR UNTIL LIGHTLY GOLDEN. REDUCE HEAT TO MEDIUM AND ADD RICE, SESAME OIL, SOY SAUCE, GARLIC POWDER AND GREEN ONIONS. COOK, STIRRING OCCASIONALLY, FOR 5 TO 7 MINUTES, BREAKING UP ANY CLUMPS OF RICE. FRY UNTIL RICE IS HOT AND BEGINNING TO CRISP. REMOVE SKILLET FROM HEAT AND STIR IN BACON PIECES AND SESAME SEEDS.

MEANWHILE, IN ANOTHER SKILLET, OVER MEDIUM-HIGH HEAT, HEAT CANOLA OIL AND FRY EGGS SUNNY-SIDE-UP, TO DESIRED DONENESS. DIVIDE RICE ONTO FOUR PLATES AND TOP EACH WITH AN EGG. GARNISH WITH ADDITIONAL SESAME SEEDS, IF DESIRED. SERVES 4.

TIP: THE KEY TO GETTING THE PERFECT TEXTURE FOR THIS DISH IS TO USE LEFTOVER COOKED RICE, SINCE FRESH COOKED RICE WOULD BE TOO MOIST.

CHORIZO AND
BLACK BEANS ON RICE

*THIS SUPER SATISFYING ONE-POT MEAL
IS QUICK TO MAKE. THE FULL FLAVOR OF
CHORIZO MAKES IT EXTRA DELICIOUS.*

1 TSP	CANOLA OIL	5 ML
1	ONION, CHOPPED	1
1/2 LB	FRESH CHORIZO SAUSAGE, CASINGS REMOVED	250 G
1	RED BELL PEPPER, CHOPPED	1
1 TBSP	TACO SEASONING MIX (STORE-BOUGHT OR RECIPE ON PAGE 59)	15 ML
2	GARLIC CLOVES, MINCED	2
2	CANS (19 OZ/540 ML) BLACK BEANS, RINSED AND DRAINED	2
1	CAN (28 OZ/798 ML) DICED TOMATOES	1
	SALT AND BLACK PEPPER	
	HOT COOKED RICE	
1/2 CUP	CHOPPED FRESH CILANTRO	125 ML
1	LIME, CUT INTO WEDGES	1

IN A LARGE POT, OVER MEDIUM-HIGH HEAT, HEAT OIL. ADD
ONION, COOK, STIRRING OCCASIONALLY, FOR 3 MINUTES.
ADD CHORIZO; COOK 5 MINUTES, STIRRING AND BREAKING
INTO SMALL PIECES. ADD RED PEPPER, TACO SEASONING
AND GARLIC; COOK FOR 30 SECONDS. STIR IN BEANS AND
TOMATOES; BRING TO A SIMMER, THEN REDUCE HEAT TO
MEDIUM-LOW. COVER AND COOK 10 MINUTES, THEN ADD

SALT AND PEPPER, TO TASTE. SCOOP RICE INTO BOWLS, LADLE BEAN MIXTURE ON TOP, SPRINKLE WITH CILANTRO AND SERVE WITH LIME WEDGES ON THE SIDE. SERVES 6.

TIP: SERVE ANY HEATED LEFTOVERS IN A TORTILLA FOR A SATISFYING HOT MEAL ON THE GO.

MAKE AHEAD: COVER AND REFRIGERATE FOR UP TO 4 DAYS. MAKE A DOUBLE BATCH AND FREEZE FOR UP 2 MONTHS.

SAUSAGE AND PEPPER BUN SHEET-PAN DINNER

THIS SIMPLE SUPPER IS A FAVORITE FOR SARAH AND GREG, EMILY'S COUSINS, WHO LOVE A CLASSIC AND WANT TO EAT A GREAT MEAL WITH THEIR YOUNG FAMILY.

1	RED BELL PEPPER, SLICED	1
1	YELLOW BELL PEPPER, SLICED	1
1	SMALL ONION, SLICED	1
1 TBSP	CANOLA OIL	15 ML
1/4 TSP	EACH SALT AND BLACK PEPPER	1 ML
1	PACKAGE (1 LB/500 G) HONEY GARLIC SAUSAGES	1
3 TBSP	HONEY MUSTARD OR DIJON MUSTARD	45 ML
4	SAUSAGE OR BRIOCHE HOTDOG BUNS, SPLIT	4
1/2 CUP	SHREDDED MOZZARELLA-CHEDDAR CHEESE BLEND	125 ML

PREHEAT OVEN TO 400°F (200°C). LINE A BAKING SHEET WITH PARCHMENT PAPER.

IN A BOWL, TOSS PEPPERS AND ONION WITH OIL, SALT AND PEPPER. PLACE ON PREPARED PAN AND ADD SAUSAGES. ROAST FOR ABOUT 25 MINUTES, TURNING SAUSAGES HALFWAY THROUGH, UNTIL MEAT THERMOMETER REACHES 165°F (74°C) WHEN INSERTED INTO SAUSAGES.

SPREAD HONEY MUSTARD INSIDE SAUSAGE BUNS. TUCK A SAUSAGE INTO EACH BUN ALONG WITH PEPPERS. SPRINKLE EACH WITH SOME CHEESE AND RETURN TO

BAKING SHEET. RETURN TO OVEN FOR ABOUT 5 MINUTES OR UNTIL BUNS ARE TOASTED AND CHEESE MELTS. SERVES 4.

TIP: USE ANY OF YOUR FAVORITE FRESH SAUSAGES FOR THIS RECIPE.

LAMB MEATBALL
AND DATE TAGINE

THIS RECIPE IS A SPIN ON TRADITIONAL
MEATBALLS WITH THE FLAVORS OF A TAGINE STEW.
TOGETHER THE LAMB MEATBALLS HAVE A WONDERFUL
AROMA, AND THE HINT OF SWEETNESS FROM THE
DATES MAKES A LOVELY SAUCE TO COAT THEM.
SERVE THEM OVER COUSCOUS.

I LB	GROUND LAMB	500 G
1½ TSP	PAPRIKA	7 ML
½ TSP	SALT	2 ML
¼ TSP	GROUND GINGER	I ML
¼ TSP	GROUND TURMERIC	I ML
I TBSP	CANOLA OIL	15 ML
I	ONION, CHOPPED	I
2	GARLIC CLOVES, MINCED	2
2 TBSP	CHOPPED FRESH CILANTRO	30 ML
I CUP	TOMATO SAUCE	250 ML
I CUP	WATER	250 ML
PINCH	SAFFRON THREADS (OPTIONAL)	PINCH
I CUP	PITTED MEDJOOL DATES, CHOPPED (ABOUT 10)	250 ML

IN A LARGE BOWL, MIX TOGETHER LAMB, PAPRIKA, SALT,
GINGER AND TURMERIC. ROLL INTO ABOUT 16 MEATBALLS.

IN A SKILLET, HEAT OIL OVER MEDIUM-HIGH HEAT.
BROWN MEATBALLS ON ALL SIDES AND REMOVE TO PLATE.
REDUCE HEAT TO MEDIUM AND COOK ONION, GARLIC AND

CILANTRO FOR ABOUT 5 MINUTES OR UNTIL SOFTENED AND STARTING TO BECOME GOLDEN. POUR IN TOMATO SAUCE, WATER AND SAFFRON (IF USING) AND BRING TO A SIMMER.

RETURN MEATBALLS TO SKILLET, ADD DATES AND STIR TO COMBINE. COVER AND SIMMER FOR ABOUT 12 MINUTES OR UNTIL MEATBALLS ARE NO LONGER PINK AND SAUCE IS THICKENED. SEASON SAUCE WITH SALT, IF DESIRED. SERVES 4 TO 6.

MAKE AHEAD: LET COOL COMPLETELY AND REFRIGERATE FOR UP TO 2 DAYS. REHEAT IN SKILLET OR SAUCEPAN OVER MEDIUM-LOW HEAT. ALTERNATIVELY, FREEZE IN AN AIRTIGHT CONTAINER FOR UP TO 2 WEEKS.

HERB GARLIC-CRUSTED RACK OF LAMB

HERE'S A FAVORITE WITH GUESTS AND FAMILY TOO. THIS IS QUICK AND ELEGANT ENOUGH FOR SPECIAL OCCASIONS IF YOU WANT TO SHARE.

2	RACKS OF LAMB (ABOUT 1½ LB/750 G EACH	2
1 TSP	EACH SALT AND BLACK PEPPER	5 ML
1 TBSP	CANOLA OIL	15 ML
2 TBSP	DIJON MUSTARD	30 ML
1 CUP	FRESH BREAD CRUMBS	250 ML
3 TBSP	GRATED PARMESAN CHEESE	45 ML
2 TBSP	CHOPPED FRESH PARSLEY	30 ML
2	GARLIC CLOVES, MINCED	2
1 TSP	CHOPPED FRESH THYME OR ROSEMARY	5 ML
¼ CUP	BUTTER, MELTED	60 ML

TRIM FAT FROM LAMB RACKS, IF ANY, AND SPRINKLE ALL OVER WITH SALT AND PEPPER.

PREHEAT OVEN TO 425°F (220°C). LINE A BAKING SHEET WITH FOIL.

IN A LARGE NONSTICK SKILLET, HEAT OIL OVER MEDIUM-HIGH HEAT AND BROWN RACKS ON BOTH SIDES. REMOVE TO PREPARED BAKING SHEET, BONE SIDE DOWN. BRUSH LAMB WITH MUSTARD.

IN A BOWL, COMBINE BREAD CRUMBS, CHEESE, PARSLEY, GARLIC AND THYME. DRIZZLE BUTTER OVER TOP AND TOSS WITH FORK TO COAT. PAT BREAD CRUMB MIXTURE ONTO RACKS AND ROAST FOR ABOUT 20 MINUTES FOR RARE OR UNTIL DESIRED DONENESS. LET STAND 3 MINUTES BEFORE CUTTING INTO CHOPS TO SERVE. SERVES 4 TO 6.

TIP: YOU CAN CUT THE RACK INTO CHOPS AND BROWN THEM INDIVIDUALLY, THEN BRUSH WITH MUSTARD AND TOP THEM WITH THE BREAD CRUMB MIXTURE; REDUCE BAKING TIME TO ABOUT 10 MINUTES.

GARLIC SOY PORK TENDERLOIN

INSPIRED BY THE WONDERFUL FLAVORS OF VIETNAMESE FOOD THAT WE LOVE, WE CREATED THIS TASTY PORK DISH. SWEET AND TANGY GRILLED PORK IS DELICIOUS SERVED WITH COOKED RICE OR RICE NOODLES, ALONG WITH SLICED TOMATOES, CUCUMBERS, LETTUCE AND CILANTRO.

1	SHALLOT, FINELY DICED	1
5	GARLIC CLOVES, MINCED	5
3 TBSP	PACKED BROWN SUGAR	45 ML
2 TBSP	FISH SAUCE	30 ML
2 TBSP	SOY SAUCE	30 ML
2 TBSP	LIME JUICE	30 ML
1 TBSP	CANOLA OIL	15 ML
2 LB	PORK TENDERLOIN (ABOUT 2)	1 KG
2	GREEN ONIONS, FINELY SLICED	2

IN A RESEALABLE PLASTIC BAG, COMBINE SHALLOT, GARLIC, BROWN SUGAR, FISH SAUCE, SOY SAUCE, LIME JUICE AND OIL. ADD PORK, TURNING TO COAT; REFRIGERATE 1 HOUR OR OVERNIGHT, TURNING PORK OCCASIONALLY.

PREHEAT BARBECUE GRILL TO MEDIUM-HIGH. REMOVE PORK FROM MARINADE, DISCARDING MARINADE. GRILL 10 TO 15 MINUTES, TURNING PORK EVERY FEW MINUTES, UNTIL A MEAT THERMOMETER INSERTED IN THE THICKEST PART OF THE MEAT REGISTERS 145°F (63°C), OR TO DESIRED DONENESS. SERVES 8.

TIP: REMOVE THE TOUGH SILVERSKIN FROM THE TENDERLOIN BEFORE MARINATING.

FISH AND SEAFOOD

CREAMY TUNA
PASTA WITH PEAS

WE LOVE ONE-POT PASTA MEALS WHEN THE
PASTA COOKS TOGETHER WITH THE SAUCE. THIS
CLASSIC DISH REQUIRES NO BAKING. AND WHO
DOESN'T LOVE A CRUNCHY CHIP TOPPING?

2 TBSP	CANOLA OIL	30 ML
I	ONION, FINELY CHOPPED	I
2	CELERY STALKS, DICED	2
6 OZ	DRIED BROAD EGG NOODLES (ABOUT 3 CUPS/750 ML)	175 G
2 CUPS	READY-TO-USE CHICKEN BROTH	500 ML
I	CAN (12 OZ OR 370 ML) EVAPORATED MILK	I
2 TSP	DIJON MUSTARD	10 ML
2	CANS (EACH 6 OZ/175 G) SOLID WHITE TUNA, PACKED IN WATER, DRAINED AND BROKEN INTO BITE-SIZE CHUNKS	2
1½ CUPS	FROZEN MIXED PEAS AND CARROTS, THAWED	375 ML
¾ CUP	SHREDDED CHEDDAR CHEESE	175 ML
I CUP	CRUSHED TACO OR POTATO CHIPS	250 ML
	SALT AND BLACK PEPPER	

IN A LARGE POT, OVER MEDIUM-HIGH HEAT, HEAT OIL;
ADD ONION AND CELERY. COOK, STIRRING OCCASIONALLY,
FOR 5 MINUTES, UNTIL VEGETABLES BEGIN TO SOFTEN.
DECREASE HEAT TO MEDIUM AND STIR IN NOODLES,
BROTH, MILK AND MUSTARD. COOK, UNCOVERED, STIRRING
OCCASIONALLY UNTIL NOODLES ARE JUST TENDER,

ABOUT 12 TO 15 MINUTES. STIR IN TUNA, VEGETABLES AND
CHEESE; COOK 3 MINUTES OR UNTIL HEATED THROUGH.
SEASON TO TASTE WITH SALT AND PEPPER. SERVE
NOODLES WITH CRUSHED CHIPS SPRINKLED ON TOP.
SERVES 4 TO 5.

TIP: USE A FORK OR SPOON TO BREAK UP THE TUNA
DIRECTLY IN THE CAN.

CANNED SALMON PATTIES

*THESE PATTIES CAN BE ENJOYED COLD OR HOT!
THE VERSATILITY THIS RECIPE OFFERS YOU IS
TWOFOLD — HAVE IT AS A SALAD COLD OR
PAN-FRIED WITH RICE AND VEGGIES FOR AN
INSPIRED DINNER FROM THE PANTRY.*

1 CUP	CANNED CHICKPEAS	250 ML
2	CANS (213 G EACH) SOCKEYE SALMON, DRAINED	2
1/2 CUP	DICED CELERY	125 ML
1/2 CUP	DICED RED BELL PEPPER	125 ML
1	DILL PICKLE, FINELY DICED	1
1/3 CUP	MAYONNAISE	75 ML
1 TBSP	LEMON JUICE	15 ML
1/4 TSP	EACH SALT AND BLACK PEPPER	1 ML
8	LEAVES BOSTON OR LEAF LETTUCE	8
1	TOMATO, SLICED	1

IN A LARGE BOWL, MASH CHICKPEAS USING A POTATO MASHER. ADD SALMON AND MASH TOGETHER. STIR IN CELERY, RED PEPPER AND PICKLE.

IN A SMALL BOWL, WHISK TOGETHER MAYONNAISE, LEMON JUICE, SALT AND PEPPER. SCRAPE INTO SALMON MIXTURE AND STIR TO COMBINE WELL. (MIXTURE WILL BE SOFT.) DIVIDE SALMON MIXTURE INTO 8 PATTIES, USING ABOUT 1/2 CUP (125 ML) FOR EACH.

SPRAY LARGE NONSTICK SKILLET WITH COOKING SPRAY AND PLACE ON MEDIUM-HIGH HEAT. ADD PATTIES AND COOK FOR ABOUT 5 MINUTES PER SIDE OR UNTIL GOLDEN ON BOTH SIDES, GENTLY TURNING ONCE. PLACE PATTIES ON LETTUCE LEAVES AND TOP WITH TOMATO SLICES TO SERVE. SERVES 4.

TIP: IF YOU PREFER A FIRMER SALMON PATTY, STIR IN $1/3$ CUP (75 ML) DRY BREAD CRUMBS BEFORE SHAPING INTO PATTIES. IF YOU NEED A WHEAT-FREE OPTION, BE SURE TO USE GLUTEN-FREE BREAD CRUMBS.

GARLIC CILANTRO SHRIMP TACOS

WHAT A FUN AND EASY WAY TO ENJOY SHRIMP AND TACOS. IF YOU HAVE TEENAGERS, WATCH OUT — YOU MIGHT HAVE TO DOUBLE THE RECIPE IN ORDER TO ENJOY SOME YOURSELF! LOOK FOR THE SMALL "STREET TACO"-SIZE TORTILLAS FOR A PERFECT RATIO OF SHRIMP TO TORTILLA.

1 LB	LARGE RAW PEELED AND DEVEINED BLACK TIGER SHRIMP (31/40 COUNT)	500 G
2 TBSP	CANOLA OIL	30 ML
2 TBSP	CHOPPED FRESH CILANTRO	30 ML
2	GARLIC CLOVES, MINCED	2
2 TSP	SMOKED PAPRIKA	10 ML
1 CUP	DICED FRESH TOMATO	250 ML
1/4 TSP	SALT	1 ML
1/2 TSP	GRATED LIME ZEST	2 ML
1 TBSP	LIME JUICE	15 ML
8	SMALL CORN OR FLOUR TORTILLAS	8
1/2 CUP	SHREDDED JALAPEÑO HAVARTI OR GOUDA CHEESE	125 ML
	LIME WEDGES (OPTIONAL)	

REMOVE TAILS FROM SHRIMP. IN A LARGE BOWL, TOSS SHRIMP WITH OIL, CILANTRO, GARLIC AND PAPRIKA. LET STAND FOR 10 MINUTES.

MEANWHILE, HEAT A LARGE NONSTICK SKILLET OVER MEDIUM-HIGH HEAT; ADD TOMATOES AND SALT. COOK, STIRRING, FOR ABOUT 2 MINUTES OR UNTIL TOMATOES

START TO SOFTEN. ADD SHRIMP MIXTURE AND STIR TO COMBINE. COOK FOR ABOUT 5 MINUTES OR UNTIL SHRIMP IS PINK AND FIRM. STIR IN LIME ZEST AND JUICE AND REMOVE FROM HEAT.

DIVIDE MIXTURE AMONG TORTILLAS AND SPRINKLE EACH WITH CHEESE TO SERVE. SERVE WITH LIME WEDGE, IF DESIRED. SERVES 4.

TIP: "STREET TACO" SIZE IS ABOUT 5 INCHES (12.5 CM), AND THEY ARE AVAILABLE IN FLOUR OR CORN.

TIP: SUBSTITUTE CANNED DICED TOMATOES FOR THE FRESH IF NEEDED.

SMOKY SALMON BOWL

YOU CAN BUILD YOUR BOWL IN LAYERS OR SERVE THIS IN A SHALLOW BOWL SO THAT ALL THE INGREDIENTS HAVE THEIR OWN SPACE. IN THE END, ALL THE INGREDIENTS GET TOSSED TOGETHER BEFORE YOU DIG IN! WE HAVE A GREAT HOMEMADE TACO SEASONING MIX RECIPE ON PAGE 59, OR YOU CAN ALSO USE STORE-BOUGHT.

2 TBSP	TACO SEASONING MIX (STORE-BOUGHT OR SEE RECIPE PAGE 59)	30 ML
2 TBSP	CANOLA OIL	30 ML
6	SALMON FILLETS (ABOUT 4 OZ/ 125 G EACH)	6
3 CUPS	HOT COOKED WHITE OR BROWN RICE	750 ML
2	AVOCADOS, PEELED AND SLICED	2
1	CAN (19 OZ/540 ML) BLACK BEANS, DRAINED AND RINSED	1
1½ CUPS	CORN KERNELS	375 ML
1 CUP	SHREDDED RED CABBAGE	250 ML
1	LIME, CUT INTO WEDGES	1
	CHOPPED FRESH CILANTRO OR GREEN ONIONS	
	SALSA OR SOUR CREAM	

IN A SMALL BOWL, STIR TOGETHER TACO SEASONING AND OIL.

PREHEAT OVEN TO 425°F (220°C). LINE A BAKING SHEET WITH PARCHMENT PAPER AND PLACE SALMON ON TOP. SPREAD SEASONING MIXTURE ALL OVER SALMON FILLETS.

ROAST IN OVEN FOR 10 MINUTES, OR UNTIL FISH FLAKES WHEN TESTED.

DIVIDE RICE, AVOCADOS, BEANS, CORN, CABBAGE AND LIME AMONG SIX BOWLS, THEN TOP WITH SALMON, CILANTRO AND SALSA. SERVES 6.

TIP: CHECK AVOCADO RIPENESS BY REMOVING THE STEM CAP ON THE TOP. IF THE STEM COMES OFF EASILY, THEN IT'S READY FOR EATING.

SHEET-PAN FISH AND POLENTA CUBES

THIS SURPRISING COMBINATION WILL WIN OVER YOUR FAMILY. THE EASE OF SHEET-PAN MEALS MAKES THEM A FAVORITE AND, WITH FISH, REALLY QUICK, TOO.

1/2	2 LB (1 KG) LOG PREPARED POLENTA, CUT INTO 1-INCH (2.5 CM) CUBES	1/2
2 TBSP	EXTRA VIRGIN OLIVE OIL	30 ML
1 TSP	DRIED ITALIAN SEASONING, DIVIDED	5 ML
1/2 TSP	EACH SALT AND BLACK PEPPER, DIVIDED	2 ML
4	COD OR HADDOCK FILLETS	4
1 CUP	TOMATO BASIL PASTA SAUCE, DIVIDED	250 ML
1/2 CUP	PANKO	125 ML
2 TBSP	BUTTER, MELTED	30 ML

PREHEAT OVEN TO 425°F (220°C). LINE LARGE BAKING SHEET WITH PARCHMENT PAPER.

IN A LARGE BOWL, TOSS POLENTA CUBES WITH OIL, 1/2 TSP (2 ML) OF THE ITALIAN SEASONING AND HALF EACH OF THE SALT AND PEPPER. SPREAD ONTO HALF OF PREPARED BAKING SHEET. BAKE FOR 10 MINUTES.

MEANWHILE, SPRINKLE FISH FILLETS WITH REMAINING SALT AND PEPPER. SPREAD TOPS OF FISH FILLETS WITH 1 TBSP (15 ML) OF PASTA SAUCE ON EACH. IN A SMALL BOWL, MIX TOGETHER PANKO, BUTTER AND REMAINING

ITALIAN SEASONING. ADD FISH FILLETS TO OTHER HALF OF THE BAKING SHEET AND SPRINKLE WITH PANKO MIXTURE. RETURN TO OVEN AND ROAST FOR ABOUT 10 MINUTES OR UNTIL FISH FLAKES EASILY WHEN TESTED.

MICROWAVE OR HEAT REMAINING PASTA SAUCE IN A SMALL SAUCEPAN AND SERVE WITH FISH AND POLENTA. SERVES 4.

CASHEW SALMON AND BROCCOLI

THIS UNIQUE STIR-FRY IS A GREAT WAY
TO ENJOY SALMON WITH A TWIST!

I	BUNCH BROCCOLI, CHOPPED	I
3 TBSP	CANOLA OIL, DIVIDED	45 ML
PINCH	SALT	PINCH
1/2 CUP	CHOPPED CASHEWS OR PEANUTS	125 ML
2 TSP	MINCED FRESH GINGER	10 ML
I	LARGE GARLIC CLOVE, MINCED	I
1/4 TSP	HOT PEPPER FLAKES	1 ML
I LB	SKINLESS CENTER-CUT SALMON FILLET, CUBED	500 G
1/4 CUP	SOY SAUCE	60 ML
3 TBSP	MAPLE SYRUP OR HONEY	45 ML
I TSP	CORNSTARCH	5 ML

IN A LARGE SKILLET, HEAT I TBSP (15 ML) OF THE OIL OVER MEDIUM-HIGH HEAT. ADD BROCCOLI AND SALT; STIR FRY FOR 4 MINUTES. REMOVE TO A BOWL. RETURN SKILLET TO MEDIUM HEAT AND ADD REMAINING OIL. ADD CASHEWS, GINGER, GARLIC AND HOT PEPPER FLAKES AND STIR-FRY FOR ABOUT 2 MINUTES OR UNTIL STARTING TO BROWN. ADD SALMON AND STIR-FRY FOR 3 MINUTES. RETURN BROCCOLI TO SKILLET.

IN A BOWL, WHISK TOGETHER SOY SAUCE, MAPLE SYRUP AND CORNSTARCH. POUR INTO SKILLET AND COOK, STIRRING, UNTIL WELL COATED AND SALMON IS COOKED THROUGH. SERVES 4.

Smoked Paprika Garlic Chicken (page 119)

Kimchi Bacon Fried Rice (page 138)

Sausage and Pepper Bun Sheet-Pan Dinner (page 142)

Lamb Meatball and Date Tagine (page 144)

Creamy Tuna Pasta with Peas (page 150)

Garlic Cilantro Shrimp Tacos (page 154)

Smoky Salmon Bowl (page 156)

za (page 176)

COCONUT GREEN CURRY FISH SOUP

*THIS RECIPE IS A FAVORITE WITH SYLVIA'S FAMILY.
IT'S A FLAVORFUL COMFORT FOOD SERVED
ON ITS OWN OR OVER HOT COOKED RICE.*

1 TBSP	CANOLA OIL	15 ML
1	ONION, THINLY SLICED	1
2 TBSP	THAI GREEN CURRY PASTE	30 ML
2 TSP	GRATED FRESH GINGER	10 ML
2	GARLIC CLOVES, MINCED	2
1/2 TSP	SALT	2 ML
2 CUPS	READY-TO-USE CHICKEN BROTH	500 ML
1	CAN (14 OZ/400 ML) COCONUT MILK	1
2 TSP	GRANULATED SUGAR	10 ML
1 1/2 LB	FIRM WHITE FISH (HADDOCK, COD OR POLLOCK), CUT INTO 1 1/2-INCH (4 CM) PIECES	750 G
1	ZUCCHINI, SLICED INTO 1/4-INCH (0.5 CM) ROUNDS	1
1/2 CUP	CHOPPED FRESH THAI BASIL OR CILANTRO	125 ML

IN A LARGE SAUCEPAN, OVER MEDIUM-HIGH HEAT, HEAT OIL AND ADD ONION. COOK, STIRRING OCCASIONALLY, FOR 3 MINUTES. ADD CURRY PASTE, GINGER, GARLIC AND SALT; COOK, STIRRING, FOR 30 SECONDS. STIR IN BROTH, COCONUT MILK AND SUGAR, BRING TO A SIMMER, THEN REDUCE HEAT TO MEDIUM. ADD FISH AND ZUCCHINI, COVER AND COOK 5 MINUTES OR UNTIL FISH FLAKES WHEN TESTED WITH FORK. STIR IN BASIL. SERVES 4 TO 6.

POACHED COD AND TOMATO PASTA

PAIRING FISH WITH PASTA IS A WAY TO ENJOY SOME CLASSIC FLAVOR COMBINATIONS THAT THE WHOLE FAMILY WILL LOVE. HAVE SOME FUN AND TRY SOME NEW SHORT PASTA SHAPES FOR THIS ONE!

3 CUPS	DRIED ROTINI OR CAVATAPPI PASTA	750 ML
2 TBSP	EXTRA VIRGIN OLIVE OIL	30 ML
1	LEEK, WHITE AND LIGHT GREEN PART ONLY, THINLY SLICED	1
2	GREEN ONIONS, CHOPPED	2
2	GARLIC CLOVES, MINCED	2
1	CAN (28 OZ/796 ML) DICED TOMATOES	1
1	BAY LEAF	1
1/2 TSP	SALT	2 ML
1/4 TSP	HOT PEPPER FLAKES	1 ML
1 LB	FRESH COD FILLETS, CUT INTO CHUNKS	500 G
	GRATED PARMESAN CHEESE (OPTIONAL)	

IN A POT OF BOILING SALTED WATER, COOK PASTA FOR ABOUT 8 MINUTES OR UNTIL AL DENTE. DRAIN AND RETURN TO POT; SET ASIDE.

MEANWHILE, IN A LARGE SAUCEPAN, HEAT OIL OVER MEDIUM HEAT AND COOK LEEK, ONIONS AND GARLIC FOR ABOUT 8 MINUTES OR UNTIL SOFTENED AND STARTING TO BROWN. ADD TOMATOES, BAY LEAF, SALT AND HOT PEPPER FLAKES AND BRING TO BOIL. BOIL GENTLY FOR ABOUT 10 MINUTES OR UNTIL SLIGHTLY THICKENED.

ADD COD TO TOMATO MIXTURE AND STIR GENTLY. COOK UNCOVERED, STIRRING OCCASIONALLY, FOR ABOUT 6 MINUTES OR UNTIL COD FLAKES WHEN TESTED WITH FORK AND SAUCE HAS THICKENED. STIR IN PASTA TO COAT AND WARM THROUGH. SPRINKLE WITH PARMESAN, IF DESIRED. SERVES 4.

TIP: LOOKING FOR A SPICIER VERSION? INCREASE THE HOT PEPPER FLAKES TO $\frac{1}{2}$ TSP (2 ML).

TIP: ADD I CUP (250 ML) OF PEAS IN WITH THE COD FOR SOME ADDITIONAL VEGETABLES AND TO ADD A POP OF COLOR TO THE DISH.

ANYONE WHO WANTED TO SELL FISH
HAD TO GET PERMISSION FROM GRANDPA.
HE WAS KNOWN AS THE COD FATHER.

SPICED HONEY-GLAZED SALMON

THE BALANCE OF HEAT AND SWEET TASTES PERFECT ON SALMON FILETS. QUICK BROILING OF THE FISH ENSURES IT IS MOIST AND TENDER WITH A TASTY CARAMELIZED CRUST.

4	SALMON FILLETS (ABOUT 6 OZ/175 G EACH)	4
1 1/2 TBSP	LIQUID HONEY	22 ML
2 TSP	GRAINY DIJON MUSTARD	10 ML
1 TSP	SRIRACHA	5 ML
1/4 TSP	GARLIC POWDER	1 ML
1	GREEN ONION, THINLY SLICED	1

ADJUST OVEN RACK TO 6 INCHES (15 CM) BELOW THE BROILER ELEMENT; SET OVEN TO BROIL. LINE A BAKING SHEET WITH FOIL AND PLACE SALMON ON TOP; BROIL 2 MINUTES. MEANWHILE, IN A SMALL BOWL, COMBINE HONEY, MUSTARD, SRIRACHA AND GARLIC POWDER. REMOVE SALMON FROM OVEN AND BRUSH WITH HALF OF THE HONEY MIXTURE, BROIL FOR 1 MINUTE. REMOVE FROM OVEN AND BRUSH AGAIN WITH REMAINING HONEY MIXTURE. BROIL AN ADDITIONAL 1 MINUTE, OR UNTIL FISH FLAKES WHEN TESTED. SPRINKLE WITH GREEN ONION BEFORE SERVING. SERVES 4.

TIP: MIX THE GLAZE TOGETHER AND SLICE THE ONIONS IN ADVANCE; COVER THEM AND REFRIGERATE SO YOU'RE AHEAD OF THE GAME WHEN YOU'RE READY TO START COOKING.

VEGETARIAN

QUINOA, KALE AND ROASTED SQUASH SALAD

ROAST THE SQUASH WHILE THE QUINOA IS COOKING TO SPEED UP PREPARATION TIME. EMILY'S FRIEND KATE LIKES TO MAKE HER OWN BALSAMIC DRESSING FOR THIS SALAD; YOU CAN TOO!

I CUP	READY-TO-USE VEGETABLE BROTH OR WATER	250 ML
½ CUP	QUINOA	125 ML
3 CUPS	CHOPPED BUTTERNUT SQUASH	750 ML
I TBSP	CANOLA OIL	15 ML
¼ TSP	EACH SALT AND BLACK PEPPER	I ML
I	SPRIG FRESH ROSEMARY	I
I	TUB (5 OZ/142 G) BABY KALE	I
½ CUP	BALSAMIC SALAD DRESSING	125 ML
¼ CUP	DRIED CRANBERRIES	60 ML
¼ CUP	PEPITAS	60 ML
¼ CUP	CRUMBLED FETA	60 ML

PREHEAT OVEN TO 400°F (200°C). LINE A BAKING SHEET WITH PARCHMENT PAPER; SET ASIDE.

IN A SAUCEPAN, BRING BROTH TO A BOIL; ADD QUINOA, RETURN TO A BOIL, COVER AND REDUCE HEAT TO LOW. COOK FOR ABOUT 15 MINUTES OR UNTIL BROTH IS ABSORBED. REMOVE FROM HEAT. FLUFF AND LET STAND COVERED FOR 10 MINUTES. (CAN BE COVERED AND REFRIGERATED FOR UP TO 2 DAYS.)

MEANWHILE, IN A LARGE BOWL, TOSS SQUASH WITH OIL, SALT AND PEPPER. SPREAD ONTO PREPARED BAKING SHEET. PULL LEAVES FROM ROSEMARY SPRIG; SPRINKLE OVER SQUASH. BAKE FOR ABOUT 20 MINUTES OR UNTIL TENDER AND GOLDEN. SET ASIDE. (CAN BE COVERED AND REFRIGERATED FOR UP TO 2 DAYS.)

TOSS TOGETHER COOKED QUINOA, ROASTED SQUASH AND KALE. DRIZZLE WITH SOME OF THE DRESSING TO COAT. TRANSFER TO A SERVING PLATTER. SPRINKLE WITH CRANBERRIES, PEPITAS AND FETA. DRIZZLE WITH MORE DRESSING IF DESIRED TO SERVE. SERVES 6.

TIP: BE SURE TO LEAVE OUT THE FETA FOR YOUR VEGAN FRIENDS.

TIP: MAKE YOUR OWN BALSAMIC DRESSING WITH $\frac{1}{4}$ CUP (60 ML) EACH EXTRA VIRGIN OLIVE OIL AND BALSAMIC VINEGAR, $\frac{1}{2}$ TSP (2 ML) DRIED OREGANO, AND SEASON TO TASTE WITH SALT AND PEPPER. YOU CAN ALSO CHANGE IT UP AND USE YOUR FAVORITE HONEY MUSTARD OR POPPY SEED DRESSING INSTEAD.

TIP: YOU CAN SUBSTITUTE REGULAR RAW OR ROASTED PUMPKIN SEEDS FOR THE PEPITAS.

TIP: IF YOU DON'T ENJOY KALE, TRY BABY SPINACH OR BABY ARUGULA.

GARLIC MUSHROOMS ON TOASTS

LOOK FOR VARIETY PACKS OF ASSORTED MUSHROOMS THAT INCLUDE CREMINI, SHIITAKE AND OYSTER MUSHROOMS FOR A FULL MUSHROOM FLAVOR.

1 TBSP	BUTTER	15 ML
1 LB	ASSORTED MUSHROOMS, THINLY SLICED	500 G
1	SMALL ONION, MINCED	1
3	GARLIC CLOVES, MINCED	3
1 TSP	DRIED THYME	5 ML
1/2 TSP	SALT	2 ML
PINCH	BLACK PEPPER	PINCH
1/4 CUP	CREAM CHEESE, SOFTENED	60 ML
3/4 CUP	HEAVY OR WHIPPING (35%) CREAM	175 ML
1/4 CUP	CHOPPED ROASTED RED PEPPERS	60 ML
1	BATCH GARLIC-RUBBED CROSTINI (SEE RECIPE PAGE 40)	1

IN A NONSTICK SKILLET, MELT BUTTER OVER MEDIUM-HIGH HEAT AND COOK MUSHROOMS, ONION, GARLIC, THYME, SALT AND PEPPER FOR ABOUT 10 MINUTES OR UNTIL GOLDEN BROWN AND NO LIQUID REMAINS. STIR IN CREAM CHEESE AND POUR IN CREAM. REDUCE HEAT TO MEDIUM-LOW AND COOK, STIRRING ABOUT 4 MINUTES UNTIL CHEESE IS MELTED AND SAUCE IS THICKENED. REMOVE FROM HEAT AND STIR IN RED PEPPERS.

PLACE 4 CROSTINI ON EACH SERVING PLATE AND SPOON MUSHROOM MIXTURE OVER TOP TO SERVE. SERVES 6.

MUSHROOM VARIATION: YOU CAN SUBSTITUTE BUTTON OR CREMINI MUSHROOMS FOR OTHER VARIETIES.

TIP: NOT FEELING LIKE HAVING BREAD WITH YOUR MUSHROOMS? WHY NOT COOK UP 12 OZ (375 G) OF YOUR FAVORITE PASTA AND TOSS IT WITH THE HOT GARLIC MUSHROOM MIXTURE — ENJOY!

INSTANT POT WILD RICE MUSHROOM PILAF

THE WILD RICE IN THIS DISH IS WONDERFULLY NUTTY AND CHEWY. SERVE WITH A FRESH SALAD ON THE SIDE. DID YOU KNOW THAT WILD RICE IS TECHNICALLY NOT A RICE, BUT IS ACTUALLY AN AQUATIC GRASS SEED?

2 TBSP	CANOLA OIL	30 ML
I	ONION, FINELY CHOPPED	I
10 OZ	ASSORTED MUSHROOMS, SLICED	300 G
I 1/4 CUPS	READY-TO-USE VEGETABLE BROTH	300 ML
I CUP	WILD RICE BLEND	250 ML
I TSP	DRIED ITALIAN SEASONING	5 ML
I	GARLIC CLOVE, MINCED	I
1/2 TSP	BLACK PEPPER	2 ML
I CUP	FROZEN PEAS, THAWED	250 ML

IN A 6-QUART INSTANT POT, SELECT SAUTÉ. ADD OIL, ONION AND MUSHROOMS; COOK 6 MINUTES, STIRRING OCCASIONALLY, OR UNTIL MUSHROOMS HAVE RELEASED MOST OF THEIR MOISTURE. STIR IN BROTH, RICE, ITALIAN SEASONING, GARLIC AND PEPPER; COOK, STIRRING AND SCRAPING UP ANY BROWNED BITS ON THE BOTTOM OF THE POT. PRESS CANCEL AND LOCK LID; SET PRESSURE RELEASE VALVE TO SEALING. PRESS MANUAL PRESSURE COOK; SET TO HIGH FOR 30 MINUTES. (IT TAKES ABOUT 10 MINUTES TO COME TO PRESSURE.)

WHEN COOKING FINISHES, LET THE PRESSURE RELEASE NATURALLY FOR 20 MINUTES, THEN RELEASE ANY REMAINING STEAM BY MOVING THE PRESSURE RELEASE VALVE TO VENTING. PRESS CANCEL; OPEN LID, STIR IN PEAS. SERVES 3.

TIP: FRESH MUSHROOMS SUCH AS CREMINI AND SHIITAKE WOULD BE DELICIOUS IN THIS RECIPE.

MAKE AHEAD: CHOP ONIONS AND SLICE MUSHROOMS; COVER AND REFRIGERATE OVERNIGHT.

PUTTANESCA CAULIFLOWER STEAKS

THE TRADITIONAL FLAVOR OF PUTTANESCA,
A CLASSIC INTENSELY TASTY ITALIAN SAUCE THAT
IS SERVED WITH PASTA, MAKES A GREAT WEEKNIGHT
MEAL. THE RICH FLAVORS OF CAPERS, OLIVES AND
HOT PEPPER ADD SPARK TO THE CAULIFLOWER
AND CREATE A HEARTY VEGETARIAN MEAL.

CAULIFLOWER STEAKS

1	LARGE CAULIFLOWER, TRIMMED	1
3 TBSP	EXTRA VIRGIN OLIVE OIL	45 ML
2	GARLIC CLOVES, MINCED	2
1/2 TSP	SALT	2 ML
1/4 TSP	HOT PEPPER FLAKES	1 ML

PUTTANESCA SAUCE

2 TBSP	EXTRA VIRGIN OLIVE OIL	30 ML
1	SMALL ONION, DICED	1
3	GARLIC CLOVES, MINCED	3
1 TBSP	DRIED OREGANO	15 ML
1	CAN (19 OZ/540 ML) PETITE CUT STEWED TOMATOES	1
1/4 CUP	CHOPPED, PITTED, OIL-CURED BLACK OLIVES	60 ML
2 TBSP	CHOPPED FRESH ITALIAN PARSLEY	30 ML
1 TBSP	DRAINED CAPERS	15 ML
1/4 TSP	SALT	1 ML

CAULIFLOWER STEAKS: PREHEAT OVEN TO 400°F (200°C).
LINE A BAKING SHEET WITH PARCHMENT PAPER.

CUT CAULIFLOWER VERTICALLY THROUGH STEM INTO ABOUT 4 THICK "STEAKS." PLACE ON PREPARED BAKING SHEET. ADD ANY SMALLER PIECES OF CAULIFLOWER THAT MAY HAVE FALLEN OFF AS WELL. DRIZZLE CAULIFLOWER WITH OIL, GARLIC, SALT AND HOT PEPPER FLAKES. ROAST FOR ABOUT 25 MINUTES OR UNTIL GOLDEN AND TENDER.

PUTTANESCA SAUCE: MEANWHILE, IN A SKILLET, HEAT OIL OVER MEDIUM HEAT AND COOK ONION, GARLIC AND OREGANO FOR ABOUT 3 MINUTES OR UNTIL SOFTENED. ADD TOMATOES, OLIVES, PARSLEY, CAPERS AND SALT AND BRING TO BOIL. REDUCE HEAT AND SIMMER FOR ABOUT 10 MINUTES OR UNTIL VERY THICK. SPOON OVER CAULIFLOWER STEAKS TO SERVE. SERVES 4.

TIP: NO LARGE CAULIFLOWERS AVAILABLE? SIMPLY PICK UP 2 SMALLER CAULIFLOWERS INSTEAD.

TASTY TOFU AND RICE DINNER

THIS DINNER COMES TOGETHER PRETTY QUICKLY
AND ADDS A TWIST TO A REGULAR STIR-FRY WHEN
YOU COOK THE TOFU AND VEG IN THE OVEN!

2 CUPS	READY-TO-USE VEGETABLE BROTH	500 ML
I CUP	BASMATI OR JASMINE RICE	250 ML
I	HEAD BROCCOLI	I
I	PACKAGE (350 G) EXTRA-FIRM TOFU, DICED	I
I	SMALL RED ONION, SLICED	I
1/4 CUP	SOY SAUCE	60 ML
2 TBSP	SESAME OIL	30 ML
2	GARLIC CLOVES, MINCED	2
I TBSP	MINCED FRESH GINGER	15 ML
I TSP	SRIRACHA OR HOT SAUCE (OPTIONAL)	5 ML
PINCH	SALT	PINCH

IN A SAUCEPAN, BRING BROTH AND RICE TO BOIL. REDUCE
HEAT TO LOW; COVER AND COOK FOR ABOUT IO MINUTES
OR UNTIL BROTH IS ABSORBED AND RICE IS TENDER.
SET ASIDE.

PREHEAT OVEN TO 400°F (200°C). LINE A BAKING SHEET
WITH PARCHMENT PAPER.

CUT STALKS FROM BROCCOLI AND PEEL. CUT BROCCOLI
TOP INTO SMALL FLORETS AND CHOP PEELED BROCCOLI
STEM; PLACE IN A LARGE BOWL. ADD TOFU AND RED ONION.
DRIZZLE VEGETABLES AND TOFU WITH SOY SAUCE AND OIL.

ADD GARLIC, GINGER AND SRIRACHA (IF USING), AND SALT TO TASTE. TOSS WELL UNTIL EVERYTHING IS COATED.

SPREAD ONTO PREPARED BAKING SHEET. ROAST FOR ABOUT 20 MINUTES OR UNTIL GOLDEN. REMOVE FROM OVEN AND ADD RICE. STIR TOGETHER ON SHEET PAN TO COMBINE AND SERVE. SERVES 4.

TIP: FOR THE CONDIMENT LOVERS IN THE FAMILY, HAVE SOY SAUCE AND SRIRACHA AVAILABLE TO DRIZZLE MORE OVER TOP IF DESIRED.

TIP: ADDING THE RICE TO THE SHEET PAN HELPS ABSORB ALL THE WONDERFUL FLAVORS FROM THE TOFU AND VEGETABLES. AND IT'S A FUN, DIFFERENT WAY TO SERVE UP DINNER.

FLORENTINE PIZZA

TAKE SIMPLE SPINACH TO ANOTHER LEVEL WITH THIS CLASSIC PIZZA WITH A TWIST, SERVING IT UP ON NAAN BREAD. A SPLASH OF FLAVOR AND COLOR COMES FROM THE GARLIC AND BELL PEPPER.

I TBSP	CANOLA OIL	15 ML
I	SMALL ONION, DICED	I
2	GARLIC CLOVES, MINCED	2
I	SMALL RED BELL PEPPER, CHOPPED	I
2 TSP	DRIED OREGANO	IO ML
I	TUB (II OZ/3I2 G) FRESH BABY SPINACH	I
1/4 TSP	EACH SALT AND BLACK PEPPER	I ML
6	MINI NAAN BREADS	6
1/2 CUP	PIZZA OR PASTA SAUCE	125 ML
I CUP	SHREDDED MOZZARELLA CHEESE	250 ML

IN A LARGE NONSTICK SKILLET, HEAT OIL OVER MEDIUM HEAT. COOK ONION, GARLIC, RED PEPPER AND OREGANO, STIRRING FOR ABOUT 5 MINUTES OR UNTIL SOFTENED. ADD SPINACH AND COOK, STIRRING FOR ABOUT 3 MINUTES OR UNTIL SPINACH IS WILTED. DRAIN ANY WATER IF NECESSARY. STIR IN SALT AND PEPPER.

PREHEAT OVEN TO 400°F (200°C). PLACE NAAN BREADS ON LARGE BAKING SHEET AND SPREAD WITH PIZZA SAUCE. SPREAD SPINACH MIXTURE OVER TOP OF EACH BREAD. SPRINKLE WITH CHEESE. BAKE FOR ABOUT 8 MINUTES OR UNTIL CHEESE IS MELTED AND NAAN IS GOLDEN.

SERVES 4.

VEGAN OPTION: SUBSTITUTE VEGAN SHREDDED CHEESE FOR THE MOZZARELLA.

REGULAR NAAN VERSION: YOU CAN SUBSTITUTE 4 REGULAR-SIZE NAAN FOR THE 6 MINI NAAN BREADS. (MINI NAAN ARE LARGER THAN NAAN DIPPERS.)

TIP: LOOKING TO JAZZ UP THIS PIZZA? TOP IT WITH A FRIED EGG FOR SOME VEGETARIAN PROTEIN.

RUSTIC VEGGIE GALETTES

*EVEN THE MEAT LOVERS IN SYLVIA'S FAMILY
DEVOURED THIS MEAL! BROILING THE VEGETABLES
BRINGS OUT THE SWEETNESS AND FLAVOR OF
THE VEGETABLES. THE CRISP PASTRY PROVIDES
A SAVORY AND SATISFYING CRISPNESS TO
HOLD THE FLAVOR-PACKED FILLING.*

8 OZ	CREMINI MUSHROOMS, QUARTERED	250 G
I	RED BELL PEPPER, CHOPPED	I
I	ZUCCHINI, THINLY SLICED	I
I	ONION, THINLY SLICED	I
2 TBSP	CANOLA OIL	30 ML
2 TSP	BALSAMIC VINEGAR	IO ML
I TSP	DRIED ITALIAN SEASONING	5 ML
1/2 TSP	EACH SALT AND BLACK PEPPER	2 ML
I LB	FROZEN PUFF PASTRY, THAWED	500 G
1/2 CUP	SUN-DRIED TOMATO PESTO	125 ML
8 OZ	SHREDDED MONTEREY JACK CHEESE	250 G
I	LARGE EGG, LIGHTLY BEATEN	I

ADJUST THE OVEN RACK TO 6 INCHES (15 CM) BELOW
THE BROILER ELEMENT; SET OVEN TO BROIL. ON A
LARGE RIMMED BAKING SHEET, PLACE MUSHROOMS, RED
PEPPER, ZUCCHINI AND ONION. ADD OIL, VINEGAR, ITALIAN
SEASONING, SALT AND PEPPER. TOSS TO COAT EVENLY,
THEN SPREAD IN A SINGLE LAYER. BROIL 12 TO 15 MINUTES,
UNTIL VEGETABLES ARE TENDER AND BROWNED ON THE
EDGES. REMOVE BAKING SHEET FROM OVEN AND SET ON

A RACK TO COOL FOR 10 MINUTES. TURN BROILER OFF AND CAREFULLY MOVE THE OVEN RACKS TO THE UPPER AND LOWER THIRD POSITIONS. SET OVEN TO 425°F (220°C).

SET ASIDE TWO PARCHMENT PAPER LINED BAKING SHEETS. DIVIDE PASTRY IN TWO. ON A LIGHTLY FLOURED SURFACE, ROLL OUT ONE PIECE OF THE PASTRY INTO A 12-INCH (30 CM) CIRCLE, THEN TRANSFER ONTO THE PREPARED BAKING SHEET. SPREAD THE PASTRY WITH HALF OF THE PESTO, THEN TOP WITH HALF OF THE CHEESE. SPOON HALF OF THE VEGETABLES ONTO THE CENTER OF THE PASTRY, MOUNDING SLIGHTLY, LEAVING A 2-INCH (5 CM) BORDER. GENTLY FOLD UP THE PASTRY EDGE AROUND THE FILLING, PINCHING AND PLEATING AS YOU GO AROUND. BRUSH THE PASTRY WITH EGG.

REPEAT WITH REMAINING PASTRY AND OTHER INGREDIENTS FOR SECOND GALETTE. BAKE 25 TO 30 MINUTES, OR UNTIL PASTRY IS CRISP AND GOLDEN BROWN. SWITCH BAKING SHEETS TOP TO BOTTOM HALFWAY THROUGH BAKING TIME. COOL SLIGHTLY BEFORE SLICING. SERVES 8.

TIP: THAW THE PASTRY IN THE REFRIGERATOR OVERNIGHT.

MAKE AHEAD: BROIL THE VEGETABLES A DAY AHEAD, COVER AND REFRIGERATE UNTIL READY TO USE.

POLENTA AND
CHEESE-STUFFED PEPPERS

*THIS NEW SPIN ON STUFFED PEPPERS
IS WONDERFUL AND COMFORTING.
YOU WON'T MISS THE CLASSIC.*

2 TBSP	CANOLA OIL	30 ML
1	ONION, DICED	1
1	ZUCCHINI, DICED	1
4	GARLIC CLOVES, MINCED	4
PINCH	HOT PEPPER FLAKES	PINCH
2 CUPS	READY-TO-USE VEGETABLE BROTH	500 ML
1/2 CUP	CORNMEAL	125 ML
1/4 CUP	CHOPPED FRESH PARSLEY	60 ML
1 1/2 CUPS	SHREDDED MOZZARELLA-CHEDDAR CHEESE BLEND, DIVIDED	375 ML
3	RED BELL PEPPERS, HALVED	3
1 1/2 CUPS	TOMATO BASIL PASTA SAUCE	375 ML

IN A SKILLET, HEAT OIL OVER MEDIUM HEAT. COOK
ONION, ZUCCHINI, GARLIC AND HOT PEPPER FLAKES FOR
5 MINUTES OR UNTIL SOFTENED. POUR IN BROTH AND
BRING TO A BOIL. WHISK IN CORNMEAL AND COOK ON LOW
HEAT, STIRRING, FOR ABOUT 15 MINUTES OR UNTIL VERY
THICK. STIR IN PARSLEY; REMOVE FROM HEAT. STIR IN
1 CUP (250 ML) OF THE CHEESE.

PREHEAT OVEN TO 400°F (200°C).

POUR PASTA SAUCE INTO BOTTOM OF 11- BY 7-INCH (28 BY 18 CM) CASSEROLE DISH. SPOON POLENTA FILLING INTO PEPPER HALVES AND PLACE INTO CASSEROLE DISH. COVER WITH FOIL AND BAKE FOR ABOUT 35 MINUTES OR UNTIL PEPPERS ARE TENDER. UNCOVER AND SPRINKLE WITH REMAINING CHEESE AND BAKE FOR 10 MINUTES OR UNTIL CHEESE IS GOLDEN AND BUBBLY. SERVES 6.

MAKE AHEAD: BEFORE BAKING, COVER THE CASSEROLE DISH AND REFRIGERATE FOR UP TO 1 DAY. ADD ABOUT 10 MINUTES TO THE OVEN TIME WHEN REHEATING.

MISO-GLAZED EGGPLANT

THIS IS DELICIOUS SERVED ON TOP OF COOKED
RICE OR QUINOA. MAKING DIAGONAL CUTS IN THE
EGGPLANT CREATES POCKETS FOR THE GLAZE,
WHICH MEANS MORE FLAVOR IN EVERY BITE.

2	EGGPLANTS (2 LB/1 KG TOTAL)	2
1 TBSP	CANOLA OIL	15 ML
2 TBSP	WHITE MISO (SHIRO MISO)	30 ML
1 TBSP	PACKED BROWN SUGAR	15 ML
1 TSP	CIDER VINEGAR	5 ML
1 TSP	SOY SAUCE	5 ML
1 TSP	SESAME OIL	5 ML
1	GREEN ONION, THINLY SLICED	1
2 TSP	TOASTED SESAME SEEDS	10 ML

PREHEAT OVEN TO 450°F (230°C); SET ASIDE A PARCHMENT
PAPER LINED BAKING SHEET. CUT EACH EGGPLANT INTO
4 LENGTHWISE SLICES AND SCORE CRISSCROSS MARKS
ON THE CUT SIDE. BRUSH WITH CANOLA OIL AND BAKE
15 MINUTES, UNTIL TENDER. REMOVE FROM OVEN AND
ARRANGE OVEN RACK 6 INCHES (15 CM) BELOW THE
BROILER ELEMENT; SET OVEN TO BROIL.

MEANWHILE, IN A SMALL BOWL, COMBINE MISO, BROWN
SUGAR, VINEGAR, SOY SAUCE AND SESAME OIL. SPOON
MIXTURE ONTO CUT SIDE OF EGGPLANT AND BROIL ABOUT
3 TO 4 MINUTES, UNTIL GOLDEN AND BUBBLY. SPRINKLE
WITH GREEN ONION AND SESAME SEEDS BEFORE SERVING.
SERVES 4.

BARLEY LENTIL PEPPER STEW

THE INSTANT POT HELPS MAKE THIS HEARTY AND FLAVORFUL MEAL QUICK AND EASY TO PREPARE. BE SURE TO RINSE AND DRAIN THE LENTILS BEFORE COOKING.

2 TBSP	CANOLA OIL	30 ML
1	ONION, CHOPPED	1
2	RED BELL PEPPERS, CHOPPED	2
3 CUPS	COARSELY CHOPPED MUSHROOMS	750 ML
1/2 TSP	EACH SALT AND BLACK PEPPER	2 ML
4 CUPS	READY-TO-USE VEGETABLE BROTH	1 L
1/2 CUP	PEARL BARLEY	125 ML
1/2 CUP	DRIED GREEN OR BROWN LENTILS	125 ML
2 TBSP	TOMATO PASTE	30 ML
3	GARLIC CLOVES, MINCED	3
1 TSP	DRIED ITALIAN SEASONING	5 ML
1/2 CUP	CHOPPED FRESH PARSLEY	125 ML

IN A 6-QUART INSTANT POT, SELECT SAUTÉ. ADD OIL, ONION, RED PEPPERS, MUSHROOMS, SALT AND PEPPER; COOK, STIRRING OCCASIONALLY FOR 5 MINUTES. STIR IN BROTH, BARLEY, LENTILS, TOMATO PASTE, GARLIC AND ITALIAN SEASONING, SCRAPING UP ANY BROWNED BITS IN BOTTOM OF POT. PRESS CANCEL AND LOCK LID; SET PRESSURE VALVE TO SEALING. PRESS MANUAL PRESSURE COOK; SET TO HIGH FOR 15 MINUTES. WHEN COOKING FINISHES, QUICK-RELEASE THE STEAM BY MOVING PRESSURE RELEASE VALVE TO VENTING. PRESS CANCEL, OPEN LID AND STIR IN PARSLEY. SERVES 4 TO 5.

INSTANT POT BUTTERNUT SQUASH RISOTTO

THE CREAMY TEXTURE OF THIS RISOTTO IS WHAT COMFORT IS ALL ABOUT. USING FROZEN DICED BUTTERNUT SQUASH IS A BIG TIME-SAVER — THERE'S NO CHOPPING OR PEELING REQUIRED.

2 TBSP	CANOLA OIL	30 ML
I	ONION, FINELY CHOPPED	I
2 CUPS	ARBORIO RICE	500 ML
3	GARLIC CLOVES, MINCED	3
1/2 CUP	WHITE WINE	125 ML
3 CUPS	FROZEN DICED BUTTERNUT SQUASH	750 ML
3 1/2 CUPS	READY-TO-USE VEGETABLE BROTH	875 ML
I TBSP	DRIED SAGE	15 ML
3/4 CUP	GRATED PARMESAN CHEESE	175 ML
3 TBSP	BUTTER	45 ML
	SALT AND BLACK PEPPER	

IN A 6-QUART INSTANT POT, SELECT SAUTÉ. ADD OIL AND ONION; COOK 3 MINUTES, STIRRING OCCASIONALLY. ADD RICE AND GARLIC; COOK, STIRRING, FOR 30 SECONDS. ADD WINE, SCRAPING UP ANY BITS STUCK TO THE BOTTOM OF THE POT. STIR IN SQUASH, BROTH AND SAGE. PRESS CANCEL AND LOCK LID; SET PRESSURE RELEASE VALVE TO SEALING. PRESS MANUAL PRESSURE COOK; SET TO HIGH FOR 7 MINUTES. (IT TAKES ABOUT 10 MINUTES TO COME TO PRESSURE.) WHEN COOKING FINISHES; QUICK-RELEASE THE STEAM BY MOVING THE PRESSURE

RELEASE VALVE TO VENTING. PRESS CANCEL. OPEN LID AND ADD PARMESAN AND BUTTER; STIR VIGOROUSLY UNTIL CHEESE MELTS AND SQUASH BEGINS TO BREAK DOWN. SEASON TO TASTE WITH SALT AND PEPPER.

THE RISOTTO WILL CONTINUE TO THICKEN AS IT SITS. IF IT BECOMES TOO THICK, STIR IN A LITTLE HOT WATER TO DESIRED CONSISTENCY. SERVES 4 TO 5.

TIP: YOU CAN SUBSTITUTE 3 TBSP (45 ML) CHOPPED FRESH SAGE LEAVES FOR THE 1 TBSP (15 ML) DRIED SAGE.

TIP: FOR ADDED CRUNCH AND TEXTURE, TOP WITH TOASTED PECANS OR PUMPKIN SEEDS.

TIP: IF YOU LOVE PARMESAN CHEESE, ADD A GENEROUS SPRINKLE ON TOP OF THE RISOTTO.

CURRYWURST

CURRYWURST IS A POPULAR GERMAN STREET
CONDIMENT. IT'S A FLAVORFUL CURRY KETCHUP
SERVED ON TOP OF A SAUSAGE; WE'VE USED A
PLANT-BASED SAUSAGE IN OUR RECIPE FOR OUR
VEGETARIAN FRIENDS. YOU CAN ENJOY THIS IN A BUN
OR SERVED WITH HOT CRISPY FRENCH FRIES.

1 CUP	KETCHUP	250 ML
2 TBSP	CURRY POWDER	30 ML
1 TBSP	VEGAN WORCESTERSHIRE SAUCE	15 ML
2 TSP	SMOKED PAPRIKA	10 ML
2 TSP	ONION POWDER	10 ML
1 TSP	SRIRACHA	5 ML
1/4 TSP	GRANULATED SUGAR	1 ML
1/2 TSP	CANOLA OIL	2 ML
4	VEGETARIAN PLANT-BASED SAUSAGES (SUCH AS BRATWURST)	4
4	HOTDOG BUNS OR ROLLS	4

IN A MEDIUM POT, OVER MEDIUM HEAT, ADD KETCHUP,
CURRY, WORCESTERSHIRE, PAPRIKA, ONION POWDER,
SRIRACHA AND SUGAR. COOK, STIRRING OCCASIONALLY,
FOR 5 MINUTES. MAKES ABOUT 1 CUP (250 ML).

MEANWHILE, IN A SKILLET, OVER MEDIUM HEAT, HEAT
OIL, THEN ADD SAUSAGES. COOK UNTIL CRISP AND GOLDEN,
TURNING OCCASIONALLY UNTIL HEATED THROUGH. CUT
INTO BITE-SIZED PIECES IF DESIRED.

DRIZZLE SAUSAGES WITH SAUCE AND SPRINKLE ADDITIONAL CURRY POWDER ON TOP FOR EXTRA FLAVOR. SERVE IN OR WITH A BUN ON THE SIDE. SERVES 4.

TIP: BALSAMIC VINEGAR IS A GOOD SUBSTITUTE FOR THE WORCESTERSHIRE SAUCE IN THIS RECIPE.

JERK MUSHROOM HAND PIES

SYLVIA'S FAMILY LOVES THIS TAKE ON A
JAMAICAN CLASSIC. THE PASTRY FOR THESE
GOLDEN, SPICY MUSHROOM-FILLED PIES IS MADE IN
A FOOD PROCESSOR AND IS EASY TO WORK WITH.

PASTRY

1 1/2 CUPS	ALL-PURPOSE FLOUR	375 ML
1/2 CUP	BUTTER, SOFTENED	125 ML
1/2 CUP	CREAM CHEESE, SOFTENED	125 ML
1 TBSP	GROUND TURMERIC	15 ML

FILLING

2 TBSP	CANOLA OIL	30 ML
1	ONION, FINELY CHOPPED	1
3 CUPS	SLICED MUSHROOMS	750 ML
3	GARLIC CLOVES, MINCED	3
1 TBSP	JAMAICAN JERK SPICE MIX OR PASTE	15 ML
1 TBSP	CORNSTARCH	15 ML
1 1/2 CUPS	FROZEN MIXED VEGETABLES (CARROTS, PEAS AND CORN), THAWED	375 ML
2 TSP	SOY SAUCE	10 ML

IN THE BOWL OF A FOOD PROCESSOR, ADD FLOUR,
BUTTER, CREAM CHEESE AND TURMERIC; PULSE UNTIL
COMBINED AND A BALL BEGINS TO FORM, ABOUT 1 MINUTE.
SHAPE DOUGH INTO A DISC; WRAP IN PLASTIC WRAP AND
REFRIGERATE 30 MINUTES.

IN A LARGE SKILLET, OVER MEDIUM-HIGH HEAT, HEAT
OIL AND ADD ONION AND MUSHROOMS; COOK, STIRRING

OCCASIONALLY FOR 8 MINUTES. REDUCE HEAT TO MEDIUM, STIR IN GARLIC, JERK SPICE AND CORNSTARCH; COOK I MINUTE, STIRRING OCCASIONALLY. STIR IN VEGETABLES AND SOY SAUCE AND COOK FOR 3 MINUTES OR UNTIL VEGETABLES ARE TENDER AND MOST OF THE MOISTURE HAS EVAPORATED. REMOVE FROM HEAT AND COOL.

REMOVE DOUGH FROM THE REFRIGERATOR AND PREHEAT OVEN TO 400°F (200°C); SET ASIDE A PARCHMENT PAPER LINED BAKING SHEET. DIVIDE DOUGH INTO SIX PIECES AND ON A LIGHTLY FLOURED SURFACE ROLL OUT EACH PIECE INTO A 6-INCH (15 CM) CIRCLE. DIVIDE THE MUSHROOM MIXTURE ONTO THE CENTER OF EACH PIECE OF DOUGH. FOLD OVER TO ENCASE THE FILLING; PRESS TO SEAL AND MAKE RIDGES ALONG THE EDGE WITH THE TINES OF A FORK. TRANSFER ONTO PREPARED BAKING SHEET; THEN, USING A FORK OR KNIFE, POKE A FEW HOLES IN TOP OF EACH PATTY TO ALLOW THE STEAM TO ESCAPE. BAKE 20 MINUTES, OR UNTIL CRISP. SERVES 6.

TIP: USING THE FOOD PROCESSOR IS ALSO A SPEEDY WAY TO SLICE THE MUSHROOMS. ALTERNATIVELY, YOU CAN USE PRE-SLICED MUSHROOMS TO SAVE TIME IN PREPARATION.

TIP: TASTE FILLING AND ADD MORE SEASONING IF DESIRED.

MAKE AHEAD: THE PASTRY AND THE FILLING CAN BE MADE SEPARATELY THE DAY BEFORE. STORE IN REFRIGERATOR UNTIL READY TO USE. ALLOW THE PASTRY TO SOFTEN A LITTLE, BEFORE ROLLING OUT.

LENTILS WITH COCONUT RICE

THIS SATISFYING DISH COMES TOGETHER QUICKLY.
THE COCONUT MILK IS USED IN THE COOKING OF
BOTH THE RICE AND THE SAUCE. BE SURE TO SHAKE
OR STIR THE CONTENTS OF THE CAN OF COCONUT MILK
TO ENSURE THAT THE CREAM AND THINNER MILK
ARE WELL MIXED BEFORE USING.

RICE

1 1/2 CUPS	LONG-GRAIN WHITE RICE (JASMINE OR BASMATI), RINSED AND DRAINED	375 ML
1	CAN (14 OZ/400 ML) COCONUT MILK, STIRRED, DIVIDED	1
1 3/4 CUPS	WATER	425 ML
1/2 TSP	SALT	2 ML

LENTILS

2 TBSP	CANOLA OIL	30 ML
1	ONION, THINLY SLICED	1
2 TBSP	MINCED FRESH GINGER	30 ML
2	GARLIC CLOVES, MINCED	2
2 TBSP	MILD CURRY PASTE	10 ML
1 1/2 TBSP	GARAM MASALA	22 ML
1	CAN (28 OZ/796 ML) DICED TOMATOES	1
1	CAN (19 OZ/540 ML) LENTILS, RINSED AND DRAINED	1
2 TSP	LIQUID HONEY	10 ML
1 TSP	SALT	5 ML
3 CUPS	LIGHTLY PACKED BABY SPINACH	750 ML
1/2 CUP	CHOPPED FRESH CILANTRO, INCLUDING STEMS	125 ML

RICE: IN A MEDIUM SAUCEPAN, COMBINE RICE, 1 CUP (250 ML) COCONUT MILK, WATER AND SALT. ON HIGH HEAT, BRING MIXTURE TO BOIL, THEN REDUCE HEAT TO LOW. COVER POT; COOK FOR 15 MINUTES. REMOVE FROM HEAT AND LET SIT FOR 10 MINUTES.

LENTILS: MEANWHILE, IN A LARGE SKILLET, OVER MEDIUM-HIGH HEAT, HEAT OIL, ADD ONION AND COOK, STIRRING OCCASIONALLY, FOR 3 MINUTES. ADD GINGER, GARLIC, CURRY PASTE AND GARAM MASALA; COOK, STIRRING 30 SECONDS. STIR IN REMAINING $2/3$ CUP (150 ML) COCONUT MILK, TOMATOES, LENTILS, HONEY AND SALT; BRING MIXTURE TO A BOIL, THEN REDUCE HEAT TO MEDIUM-LOW AND SIMMER UNCOVERED FOR 15 MINUTES. STIR IN SPINACH AND COOK 1 MINUTE, UNTIL JUST WILTED. STIR IN CILANTRO. FLUFF RICE AND DIVIDE INTO BOWLS AND TOP WITH LENTIL MIXTURE. SERVES 6.

TIP: BE SURE TO USE CURRY PASTE AND NOT CURRY SAUCE FOR THIS RECIPE.

MAKE AHEAD: THIS KEEPS WELL FOR UP TO 3 DAYS IN THE REFRIGERATOR, MAKING IT A DELICIOUS MAKE-AHEAD MEAL.

ONE-SKILLET
CACIO E PEPE PASTA

*ONCE YOU MASTER THIS PASTA, YOU'LL
MAKE IT AGAIN AND AGAIN. IT'S ALMOST LIKE A
PASTA TRICK — IT'S SO EASY AND TASTES GREAT!*

8 OZ	DRIED SPAGHETTI	250 G
I TSP	SALT	5 ML
I CUP	FRESH GRATED PARMESAN CHEESE	250 ML
3 TBSP	BUTTER, AT ROOM TEMPERATURE	45 ML
	FRESH CRACKED BLACK PEPPER	

IN A LARGE HIGH-SIDED SKILLET THAT WILL FIT THE
SPAGHETTI FLAT, LAY SPAGHETTI. FILL WITH WATER
TO ABOUT $\frac{3}{4}$-INCH (2 CM) DEPTH OR TO JUST COVER
SPAGHETTI; ADD SALT. BRING TO A BOIL AND COOK,
STIRRING OCCASIONALLY, FOR ABOUT 10 MINUTES OR
UNTIL AL DENTE. WATER SHOULD HAVE REDUCED; IF
THERE IS WATER STILL IN THE SKILLET GENTLY TIP
MOST OF IT OUT INTO SINK. RETURN TO LOW HEAT
AND STIR IN BUTTER AND CHEESE UNTIL CREAMY. TOSS
WELL TO COAT AND SEASON TO TASTE WITH PEPPER.
SERVE IMMEDIATELY. SERVES 2.

Instant Pot Butternut Squash Risotto (page 184)

Jerk Mushroom Hand Pies (page 188)

Roasted Potatoes with Herb Yogurt Sauce (page 202)

Cauliflower Gremolata (variation, page 206)

Deluxe Hazelnut Shortbread Bars (page 222)

Jillian's Coconut Panna Cotta with Raspberry Chia Jam (page 225)

Freezer Strawberry Ice Cream Cheesecakes (page 236)

Toffee Brownie Trifle (page 238) with Hot Fudge Sauce (page 239)

SIDES

GARLIC NOODLES

THE INGREDIENTS IN THESE NUTTY, SWEET AND SALTY NOODLES MAY SOUND LIKE AN UNUSUAL COMBINATION, BUT ONCE YOU'VE TASTED THEM, YOU'LL BE WANTING MORE. THIS IS A BOWL OF COMFORT FOOD THAT TAKES VERY LITTLE TIME TO PREPARE.

12 OZ	DRIED SPAGHETTI	375 G
1 TBSP	OYSTER SAUCE	15 ML
1 TBSP	PACKED BROWN SUGAR	15 ML
2 TSP	FISH SAUCE	10 ML
2 TSP	SOY SAUCE	10 ML
2 TSP	SESAME OIL	10 ML
1/4 CUP	BUTTER	60 ML
1 TBSP	CANOLA OIL	15 ML
5	GARLIC CLOVES, MINCED	5
2 TBSP	FINELY GRATED PARMESAN CHEESE	30 ML
2	GREEN ONIONS, SLICED	2

IN A LARGE POT OF BOILING SALTED WATER, COOK SPAGHETTI FOR ABOUT 8 MINUTES OR UNTIL AL DENTE. RESERVE 1/2 CUP (125 ML) PASTA WATER, THEN DRAIN PASTA AND RETURN TO POT, COVER AND KEEP WARM.

WHILE THE PASTA IS COOKING, IN A SMALL BOWL, COMBINE OYSTER SAUCE, BROWN SUGAR, FISH SAUCE, SOY SAUCE AND SESAME OIL; SET ASIDE. IN A LARGE NONSTICK SKILLET, OVER LOW HEAT, HEAT BUTTER AND OIL UNTIL BUTTER MELTS, ABOUT 1 MINUTE. ADD GARLIC AND COOK 1 MINUTE OR UNTIL FRAGRANT (YOU DON'T

WANT THE GARLIC TO BROWN); STIR IN SAUCE MIXTURE. ADD PASTA AND TOSS UNTIL EVENLY COATED, ADDING A LITTLE RESERVED PASTA WATER IF NEEDED. REMOVE FROM HEAT, ADD CHEESE AND GREEN ONIONS, TOSS TO COMBINE. SERVE IMMEDIATELY. SERVES 4 TO 5.

TIP: DRIED LO MEIN EGG NOODLES CAN BE SUBSTITUTED FOR THE SPAGHETTI. COOK ACCORDING TO PACKAGE DIRECTIONS.

I LOVE HOW IN HORROR MOVIES THE PERSON WILL ASK, "IS ANYONE THERE?" AS IF THE KILLER WOULD SAY "OH YEAH, I'M IN THE KITCHEN. WANT A SANDWICH?"

SPANISH RICE

THIS EASY ONE-POT RICE IS A CLASSIC
EVERY COOK SHOULD KNOW HOW TO MAKE.
IT MAKES A GREAT SIDE DISH FOR ANY MEAL!

2 TBSP	CANOLA OIL	30 ML
1	SMALL ONION, FINELY CHOPPED	1
2	GARLIC CLOVES, MINCED	2
1	JALAPEÑO PEPPER, SEEDED AND MINCED	1
1/4 TSP	SALT	1 ML
1 CUP	LONG-GRAIN RICE	250 ML
2	VINE-RIPENED TOMATOES, CHOPPED	2
2 CUPS	READY-TO-USE VEGETABLE BROTH	500 ML

IN A SAUCEPAN, HEAT OIL OVER MEDIUM HEAT. COOK, ONION, GARLIC, JALAPEÑO AND SALT FOR ABOUT 5 MINUTES OR UNTIL SOFTENED. STIR IN RICE TO COAT. STIR IN TOMATOES AND POUR IN BROTH. BRING TO A SIMMER; COVER AND REDUCE HEAT TO LOW. COOK FOR ABOUT 20 MINUTES OR UNTIL RICE IS TENDER AND BROTH IS ABSORBED. SERVES 4.

KALE PESTO PASTA

THIS TASTY SIDE DISH CAN DOUBLE AS A MEATLESS MEAL OPTION. THE PESTO IS ALSO GREAT SPREAD ON PIZZA OR ADDED TO LIVEN UP BASIC VEGETABLES.

3/4 CUP	TOASTED WALNUT PIECES	175 ML
3	GARLIC CLOVES, PEELED	3
I TBSP	LEMON JUICE	15 ML
1 1/2 TSP	SALT	7 ML
1/2 TSP	BLACK PEPPER	2 ML
3 CUPS	PACKED KALE LEAVES (ABOUT I SMALL BUNDLE, STEMS REMOVED)	750 ML
3/4 CUP	GRATED PARMESAN CHEESE	175 ML
1/3 CUP	EXTRA-VIRGIN OLIVE OIL	75 ML
12 OZ	DRIED PASTA, SUCH AS SPAGHETTI	375 G

IN THE BOWL OF A FOOD PROCESSOR, ADD WALNUTS, GARLIC, LEMON JUICE, SALT AND PEPPER; PROCESS UNTIL CRUMBLY. SCRAPE DOWN SIDES OF BOWL; ADD KALE AND CHEESE. WITH THE MACHINE RUNNING, SLOWLY DRIZZLE IN OIL. PROCESS TO DESIRED CONSISTENCY, SCRAPING DOWN SIDES IF NECESSARY.

COOK PASTA FOR ABOUT 8 MINUTES OR UNTIL AL DENTE. RESERVE 1/2 CUP (125 ML) OF PASTA COOKING LIQUID, DRAIN PASTA AND RETURN TO POT. MIX IN ENOUGH PESTO SO IT TASTES GOOD; ADD RESERVED COOKING LIQUID IF NEEDED. SERVES 4 TO 5.

TIP: SERVE WITH ADDITIONAL PARMESAN AND PEPPER ON THE SIDE.

QUICK HERBED FLATBREAD

*USING CONVENIENT READY-MADE PIZZA DOUGH
IS A FUSS-FREE WAY TO GET THE COMFORTING
SCENT OF FRESH BAKED BREAD WAFTING THROUGH
THE HOUSE. FRESH PIZZA DOUGH IS SOLD IN BAGS
IN THE COOLER SECTION OF YOUR GROCERY STORE.*

3 TBSP	EXTRA VIRGIN OLIVE OIL, DIVIDED	45 ML
I LB	PIZZA DOUGH, ROOM TEMPERATURE	500 G
2 TSP	DRIED ITALIAN SEASONING	10 ML
1/4 TSP	SEA SALT	I ML

IN A 13- BY 9-INCH (33 BY 23 CM) BAKING PAN, SPREAD
2 TBSP (30 ML) OIL AND PLACE DOUGH. FLIP THE DOUGH
OVER A FEW TIMES SO IT IS FULLY COATED IN OIL. USE
YOUR HANDS TO PRESS AND STRETCH THE DOUGH OUT
INTO A ROUGH RECTANGLE SHAPE; COVER WITH PLASTIC
WRAP AND LEAVE TO REST 15 MINUTES. STRETCH THE
DOUGH AGAIN, THEN DRIZZLE WITH REMAINING I TBSP
(15 ML) OIL, COATING DOUGH EVENLY. WITH FINGERTIPS,
CREATE DIMPLES IN DOUGH, THEN SPRINKLE THE
ITALIAN SEASONING AND SALT OVER TOP. COVER AND
LET REST 15 MINUTES.

MEANWHILE, PREHEAT OVEN TO 450°F (230°C).
BAKE BREAD 15 TO 18 MINUTES, UNTIL GOLDEN BROWN
AND BOTTOM IS CRISP. REMOVE FROM OVEN AND
DRIZZLE WITH ADDITIONAL OIL, IF DESIRED; LET COOL
A FEW MINUTES BEFORE SERVING. SERVES 6.

MAKE AHEAD: FLATBREAD CAN BE MADE A DAY AHEAD. COOL COMPLETELY AND STORE IN AN AIRTIGHT CONTAINER. REHEAT IN A 350°F (180°C) OVEN FOR 10 MINUTES. BREAD CAN BE FROZEN FOR UP TO 1 MONTH.

TIP: SERVE ALONGSIDE SOUP, SALAD OR DIPPED INTO OLIVE OIL AND BALSAMIC VINEGAR.

GARLICKY CHEESE BUNS

THIS IS ONE OF SYLVIA'S FAMILY'S NEW FAVORITE THINGS TO EAT. MORE IS MORE WITH THESE ULTRA-CHEESY GARLICKY BUNS. YOU CAN PULL THE ROLLS APART WHILE THEY'RE WARM (WHEN THE CHEESE IS NO LONGER MOLTEN) OR CUT INTO WEDGES WHEN COOLED — IF YOU CAN WAIT THAT LONG!

1/4 CUP	MELTED BUTTER	60 ML
1 TSP	GARLIC POWDER	5 ML
1/2 TSP	ONION POWDER	2 ML
1/2 TSP	SALT	2 ML
1 LB	PIZZA DOUGH, ROOM TEMPERATURE	500 G
4 CUPS	SHREDDED SHARP (OLD) CHEDDAR CHEESE	1 L

IN A SMALL BOWL, COMBINE BUTTER, GARLIC POWDER, ONION POWDER AND SALT; SET ASIDE. LINE A 9-INCH (23 CM) ROUND CAKE PAN WITH PARCHMENT PAPER; SET ASIDE.

ON A LIGHTLY FLOURED SURFACE, ROLL DOUGH OUT IN A 13- BY 9-INCH (32.5 BY 23 CM) RECTANGLE. BRUSH WITH HALF OF THE BUTTER MIXTURE; SPRINKLE WITH 2 CUPS (500 ML) CHEESE. STARTING AT THE LONG SIDE, ROLL UP TIGHTLY INTO A LOG, PINCH THE EDGE OF THE ROLL TO SEAL. CUT CROSSWISE INTO 8 EQUAL PIECES AND PLACE IN PREPARED PAN, CUT SIDE UP. COVER WITH PLASTIC WRAP AND LET RISE IN A WARM PLACE FOR 30 MINUTES, OR UNTIL ALMOST DOUBLE IN SIZE.

PREHEAT OVEN TO 375°F (190°C). REMOVE PLASTIC WRAP FROM BUNS AND DRIZZLE WITH REMAINING BUTTER MIXTURE. (RE-WARM IF MIXTURE HAS SOLIDIFIED.) BAKE 20 MINUTES.

REMOVE FROM OVEN AND SPRINKLE WITH REMAINING 2 CUPS (500 ML) CHEESE AND BAKE ANOTHER 8 MINUTES, OR UNTIL CHEESE IS MELTED AND BEGINNING TO BROWN. COOL IN PAN ON A WIRE RACK. SERVES 8.

TIP: BREAD CAN ALSO BE BAKED IN AN 8-INCH (20 CM) SQUARE CAKE PAN.

TIP: STORE ANY LEFTOVERS IN THE REFRIGERATOR.

ROASTED POTATOES WITH HERB YOGURT SAUCE

ROASTED POTATOES ARE EXTRA DELICIOUS
SERVED WITH THIS CREAMY, HERBY, GARLICKY
FRESH SAUCE. USING TWO BAKING SHEETS
ENSURES THAT THE POTATOES HAVE PLENTY
OF SPACE TO BECOME WONDERFULLY CRISPY.

POTATOES

2 LB	MINI POTATOES, HALVED	1 KG
2 TBSP	CANOLA OIL	30 ML
1 TSP	SALT	5 ML
1/2 TSP	BLACK PEPPER	2 ML

SAUCE

1 CUP	PLAIN GREEK YOGURT	250 ML
1/4 CUP	CHOPPED FRESH HERBS SUCH AS DILL, PARSLEY, GREEN ONIONS, CILANTRO	60 ML
1 TBSP	EXTRA VIRGIN OLIVE OIL	15 ML
2 TSP	GRATED LEMON ZEST	10 ML
2	GARLIC CLOVES, MINCED	2

POTATOES: PREHEAT OVEN TO 450°F (230°C). SET
ASIDE TWO RIMMED BAKING SHEETS. IN A LARGE BOWL,
COMBINE POTATOES, OIL, SALT AND PEPPER; TOSS
TO COAT EVENLY. DIVIDE POTATOES ONTO BAKING
SHEETS, SPREADING IN A SINGLE LAYER. BAKE 25 TO
30 MINUTES, UNTIL POTATOES ARE TENDER AND CRISP
ON THE OUTSIDE.

SAUCE: MEANWHILE, IN A MEDIUM BOWL, COMBINE YOGURT, HERBS, OLIVE OIL, LEMON ZEST AND GARLIC. SEASON TO TASTE WITH SALT AND PEPPER. SERVE POTATOES WARM WITH THE HERB SAUCE. SERVES 4 TO 5.

TIP: THE YOGURT SAUCE CAN BE MADE A DAY AHEAD. COVER AND REFRIGERATE UNTIL READY TO USE.

TIP: FEEL FREE TO USE A COMBINATION OF SEVERAL FRESH HERBS.

— SKILLET-ROASTED CARROTS —

IF YOU'RE LOOKING FOR A NEW TWIST ON CARROTS, THEN YOU'LL ENJOY THIS DISH. WE'VE TOSSED THE CARROTS IN A FLAVORFUL GLAZE, THEN FINISHED WITH A TOPPING OF PARSLEY AND ZA'ATAR. ROASTING CARROTS INTENSIFIES THEIR NATURAL SWEETNESS.

1 LB	CARROTS, PEELED AND SLICED INTO 1/4-INCH (0.5 CM) STICKS	500 G
2 TBSP	CANOLA OIL	30 ML
1 TBSP	LIQUID HONEY	15 ML
1 TSP	LEMON JUICE	5 ML
1/2 TSP	GARLIC POWDER	2 ML
1/2 TSP	SALT	2 ML
2 TBSP	CHOPPED FRESH PARSLEY	30 ML
2 TSP	ZA'ATAR SPICE MIX	10 ML

PREHEAT OVEN TO 400°F (200°C). IN A LARGE OVENPROOF OR CAST-IRON SKILLET, PLACE CARROTS AND ADD OIL, HONEY, LEMON JUICE, GARLIC POWDER AND SALT. TOSS TO COAT EVENLY, THEN SPREAD OUT IN SKILLET. COVER SKILLET WITH FOIL AND BAKE 25 TO 30 MINUTES OR UNTIL CARROTS ARE FORK-TENDER. TRANSFER CARROTS TO SERVING PLATTER AND SPRINKLE WITH PARSLEY AND ZA'ATAR. SERVES 4.

TIP: TO SPEED UP PREP TIME, USE THIN, LONG BABY CARROTS AND SKIP THE STEP OF PEELING AND SLICING.

GREEN BEAN AND GARLIC SALAD

THIS EASY SIDE-DISH SALAD IS PERFECT TO
SERVE WITH GRILLED MEATS OR VEGETABLES.

1 LB	GREEN BEANS, TRIMMED	500 G
3 TBSP	RED WINE VINEGAR	45 ML
2 TBSP	EXTRA VIRGIN OLIVE OIL	30 ML
2	GARLIC CLOVES, SLICED	2
2 TBSP	CHOPPED FRESH MINT OR BASIL	30 ML
1/2 TSP	SALT	2 ML
1/4 TSP	BLACK PEPPER	1 ML

IN A LARGE SAUCEPAN OF BOILING SALTED WATER, COOK
GREEN BEANS FOR 5 TO 8 MINUTES OR UNTIL TENDER;
DRAIN WELL. RINSE UNDER COLD WATER.

MAKE-AHEAD: WRAP GREEN BEANS IN TOWEL AND PLACE IN
A PLASTIC BAG; REFRIGERATE FOR UP TO 24 HOURS.

IN A LARGE BOWL, WHISK TOGETHER VINEGAR, OIL,
GARLIC, MINT, SALT AND PEPPER. ADD BEANS AND TOSS
TO COAT. LET STAND FOR 10 MINUTES BEFORE SERVING.
SERVES 4.

TIP: IF YOU HAVE A CAN OF TUNA IN YOUR PANTRY, DRAIN
IT AND STIR IT IN WITH THE BEANS; YOU MAY HAVE
FOUND A NEW FAVORITE LUNCH SALAD.

BROCCOLI GREMOLATA

THIS LEMONY SIDE DISH IS AN EXCELLENT ADDED TOUCH TO YOUR FISH OR SEAFOOD MEAL. FRESH LEMON ZEST AND PARSLEY MAKE THE GREMOLATA REFRESHING, WHILE COOKING THE GARLIC SOFTENS IT FOR THOSE WHO ARE NOT FANS OF RAW GARLIC.

I	BUNCH BROCCOLI	I
3 TBSP	EXTRA VIRGIN OLIVE OIL	45 ML
I	LARGE GARLIC CLOVE, MINCED	I
I TBSP	LEMON JUICE	15 ML
$1/4$ TSP	EACH SALT AND BLACK PEPPER	I ML
3 TBSP	FINELY CHOPPED FRESH PARSLEY	45 ML
I TSP	GRATED LEMON ZEST	5 ML

CUT BROCCOLI INTO 2-INCH (5 CM) FLORET PIECES. PEEL STALKS AND CUT INTO I-INCH (2.5 CM) PIECES. BRING A SAUCEPAN OF WATER TO BOIL. ADD BROCCOLI AND COOK FOR 4 MINUTES OR UNTIL BRIGHT GREEN, TENDER BUT FIRM. DRAIN WELL AND SET ASIDE.

IN A LARGE NONSTICK SKILLET, HEAT OIL OVER MEDIUM HEAT. COOK GARLIC FOR I MINUTE OR UNTIL SOFTENED. ADD LEMON JUICE AND STIR TO COMBINE. ADD BROCCOLI, SALT AND PEPPER. COOK, STIRRING FOR ABOUT 2 MINUTES OR UNTIL HEATED THROUGH.

MAKE AHEAD: COVER AND REFRIGERATE FOR UP TO 2 DAYS.

IN A SMALL BOWL, STIR TOGETHER PARSLEY AND LEMON ZEST. SPRINKLE OVER TOP OF BROCCOLI TO SERVE. SERVES 4.

CAULIFLOWER VARIATION: SUBSTITUTE CAULIFLOWER FOR BROCCOLI AS IN THE PHOTO.

UP UNTIL I BOUGHT THIS BAG OF CHIPS,
I THOUGHT THE AIR WAS FREE.

ROASTED VEGGIE PAN

THIS COMBINATION OF VEGETABLES WILL
ADD COLOR AND TEXTURE TO YOUR MEAL. SELECT
YOUR FAVORITE VEGGIES TO ROAST TOGETHER
SO EVERYONE WILL ENJOY!

2 CUPS	CHOPPED CAULIFLOWER OR BROCCOLI OR HALVED BRUSSELS SPROUTS	500 ML
1	SMALL RED ONION, SLICED OR CHOPPED	1
1	RED OR YELLOW BELL PEPPER, SLICED	1
1	ZUCCHINI, SLICED	1
2 TBSP	CANOLA OIL	30 ML
1 TBSP	CHOPPED FRESH PARSLEY OR BASIL	15 ML
1 TSP	DRIED ITALIAN SEASONING	5 ML
1/2 TSP	SALT	2 ML
1/4 TSP	BLACK PEPPER	1 ML

PREHEAT OVEN TO 400°F (200°C). LINE A BAKING SHEET
WITH PARCHMENT PAPER.

IN A LARGE BOWL, TOSS TOGETHER CAULIFLOWER,
ONION, BELL PEPPER, ZUCCHINI, OIL, PARSLEY, ITALIAN
SEASONING, SALT AND PEPPER. SPREAD ONTO PREPARED
BAKING SHEET AND ROAST FOR ABOUT 25 MINUTES OR
UNTIL TENDER AND GOLDEN BROWN. SERVES 4.

VEGETABLE OPTIONS: SUBSTITUTE YOUR FAMILY'S
FAVORITE VEGETABLES. HERE ARE A FEW TO TRY.
SUBSTITUTE CHOPPED EGGPLANT OR HALVED MUSHROOMS
FOR THE CAULIFLOWER; SUBSTITUTE REGULAR OR SWEET

ONION FOR RED ONION. USE ANY COLOR OF PEPPER OR ADD SOME SPICE AND ADD A JALAPEÑO OR CHILI PEPPER TO THE MIX.

VARIATION: LOOKING FOR A BIGGER CHANGE? OMIT CAULIFLOWER AND ZUCCHINI AND USE 1 LB (500 G) MINI POTATOES, HALVED, OR CHOPPED SQUASH OR SWEET POTATO.

BRUSSELS SPROUTS GRATIN

THIS COMFORTING GRATIN GOES WELL WITH
ROASTED OR GRILLED MEAT. BRUSSELS SPROUTS
CAN BE SHREDDED IN THE FOOD PROCESSOR OR
BY HAND, USING A GRATER OR A MANDOLINE.

½ CUP	HEAVY OR WHIPPING (35%) CREAM	125 ML
½ CUP	READY-TO-USE CHICKEN BROTH	125 ML
1 TBSP	HONEY DIJON MUSTARD	15 ML
½ TSP	EACH SALT AND BLACK PEPPER	2 ML
½ TSP	ONION POWDER	2 ML
1½ LB	BRUSSELS SPROUTS, TRIMMED AND THINLY SHREDDED	750 G
1 CUP	PANKO	250 ML
2 TBSP	GRATED PARMESAN CHEESE	30 ML
2 TBSP	BUTTER, MELTED	30 ML

PREHEAT OVEN TO 375°F (190°C), LIGHTLY OIL A 10-CUP (2 L)
CASSEROLE DISH; SET ASIDE. IN A LARGE BOWL, WHISK
TOGETHER CREAM, BROTH, MUSTARD, SALT, PEPPER
AND ONION POWDER. STIR IN BRUSSELS SPROUTS, THEN
TRANSFER INTO PREPARED CASSEROLE DISH. (IT WILL
LOOK VERY FULL, BUT WILL COOK DOWN.) IN A SMALL
BOWL, STIR TOGETHER PANKO, CHEESE AND BUTTER
AND SPRINKLE OVER BRUSSELS SPROUTS. BAKE 35 TO
40 MINUTES, UNTIL SPROUTS ARE TENDER AND TOPPING
IS GOLDEN BROWN. SERVES 8.

MAKE AHEAD: THIS DISH CAN BE ASSEMBLED THE NIGHT
BEFORE. COVER AND REFRIGERATE, THEN ADD THE TOPPING
JUST BEFORE BAKING.

CUMIN ROASTED SWEET POTATOES

USING TWO BAKING SHEETS TO ROAST
THE POTATOES ENSURES THAT THE POTATOES HAVE
PLENTY OF ROOM TO ROAST AND NOT STEAM. IF YOU
PREFER, REMOVE THE SKIN FROM THE POTATOES.

2 LB	SWEET POTATOES, CUT INTO 1/2-INCH (1 CM) CUBES	1 KG
2 TBSP	CANOLA OIL	30 ML
1 TSP	GROUND CUMIN	5 ML
1 TSP	SALT	5 ML
1/4 TSP	BLACK PEPPER	1 ML
2 TBSP	MAPLE SYRUP	30 ML
1 TBSP	LEMON JUICE	15 ML

PREHEAT OVEN TO 425°F (220°C). SET ASIDE TWO
PARCHMENT PAPER LINED RIMMED BAKING SHEETS. IN
A LARGE BOWL, COMBINE SWEET POTATOES, OIL, CUMIN,
SALT AND PEPPER; TOSS TO COAT EVENLY. SPREAD THE
POTATOES ONTO BAKING SHEETS IN A SINGLE LAYER.
BAKE FOR 20 MINUTES.

MEANWHILE, IN A SMALL BOWL, WHISK TOGETHER
MAPLE SYRUP AND LEMON JUICE. REMOVE POTATOES
FROM OVEN, DRIZZLE WITH MAPLE MIXTURE AND TOSS
TO COAT EVENLY. RETURN PANS TO OVEN AND CONTINUE
BAKING ANOTHER 10 MINUTES UNTIL POTATOES ARE
TENDER. SERVES 6 TO 8.

TIP: ENJOY ANY LEFTOVER POTATOES IN A TACO BEEF
SALAD (PAGE 58) OR SMOKY SALMON BOWL (PAGE 156).

HOISIN ROASTED BROCCOLI

*YOU MIGHT FIND YOURSELF SNACKING ON THIS
SIDE DISH BEFORE IT GETS TO THE DINNER TABLE,
BECAUSE IT'S SO TENDER, CRISPY AND DELICIOUS!*

2 TBSP	CANOLA OIL	30 ML
I TBSP	HOISIN SAUCE	15 ML
1/2 TSP	GARLIC POWDER	2 ML
1/2 TSP	BLACK PEPPER	2 ML
I LB	BROCCOLI FLORETS, CUT INTO BITE-SIZE PIECES	500 G
I TBSP	TOASTED SESAME SEEDS	15 ML

PREHEAT OVEN TO 425°F (220°C); LINE A LARGE RIMMED
BAKING SHEET WITH FOIL OR PARCHMENT PAPER.

IN A LARGE BOWL, COMBINE OIL, HOISIN, GARLIC
POWDER AND PEPPER. ADD BROCCOLI AND TOSS TO COAT
EVENLY. TRANSFER BROCCOLI TO PREPARED BAKING
SHEET AND SPREAD IN SINGLE LAYER. BAKE 20 MINUTES,
OR UNTIL BROCCOLI IS TENDER CRISP AND BEGINNING
TO BROWN. REMOVE FROM OVEN AND SPRINKLE WITH
SESAME SEEDS. SERVE IMMEDIATELY. SERVES 6.

MAKE AHEAD: COMBINE THE SAUCE INGREDIENTS, COVER
AND STORE IN THE FRIDGE UNTIL READY TO USE.

SWEETS

SWEETENED CONDENSED MILK COOKIES

THESE SOFT, CHEWY COOKIES TASTE LIKE A COMBINATION OF A SUGAR COOKIE AND A SHORTBREAD COOKIE.

1¼ CUPS	ALL-PURPOSE FLOUR	300 ML
¼ CUP	CORNSTARCH	60 ML
1 TSP	BAKING POWDER	5 ML
½ TSP	SALT	2 ML
¾ CUP	BUTTER, ROOM TEMPERATURE	175 ML
3 TBSP	GRANULATED SUGAR	45 ML
½ CUP	SWEETENED CONDENSED MILK	125 ML
1 TSP	VANILLA	5 ML

PREHEAT OVEN TO 350°F (180°C); SET ASIDE A PARCHMENT PAPER LINED BAKING SHEET. IN A MEDIUM BOWL, WHISK TOGETHER FLOUR, CORNSTARCH, BAKING POWDER AND SALT; SET ASIDE. IN A LARGE BOWL, USING AN ELECTRIC MIXER, BEAT BUTTER, SUGAR, CONDENSED MILK AND VANILLA UNTIL CREAMY. STIR IN FLOUR MIXTURE UNTIL COMBINED. USING A SMALL ICE CREAM SCOOP OR 1 TBSP (15 ML), SCOOP UP DOUGH AND ROLL INTO BALLS. PLACE BALLS ON PREPARED BAKING SHEET ABOUT 1½ INCHES (4 CM) APART; FLATTEN BALLS SLIGHTLY. BAKE 10 MINUTES, UNTIL LIGHT GOLDEN. LET COOL ON BAKING TRAY FOR 5 MINUTES, THEN TRANSFER TO A COOLING RACK. MAKES ABOUT 35 COOKIES.

TIP: TRANSFER REMAINING SWEETENED CONDENSED MILK TO A JAR OR SEALED CONTAINER AND IT WILL KEEP IN THE FRIDGE FOR UP TO 1 MONTH. IT'S DELICIOUS STIRRED INTO COFFEE, TEA, DRIZZLED ON TOAST OR FOR MAKING ANOTHER BATCH OF COOKIES.

TIP: STORE COOLED COOKIES IN AN AIRTIGHT CONTAINER, AT ROOM TEMPERATURE FOR UP TO 3 DAYS OR IN THE FREEZER FOR UP TO 2 WEEKS.

MAKE AHEAD: COOKIE DOUGH CAN BE COVERED AND STORED IN THE REFRIGERATOR FOR UP TO 2 DAYS BEFORE BAKING. UNBAKED DOUGH BALLS FREEZE UP TO 1 MONTH. BAKE FROM FROZEN, ADDING 3 TO 4 MINUTES TO BAKING TIME.

VANILLA CUPCAKES

SIMPLE CUPCAKES ARE SOMETIMES ALL YOU NEED,
AND VANILLA HITS THE SPOT! WITH OR WITHOUT
FROSTING THESE ARE PERFECT FOR ANY PARTY
OR AFTERNOON SWEET TREAT.

1¼ CUPS	ALL-PURPOSE FLOUR	300 ML
½ TSP	BAKING POWDER	2 ML
½ TSP	BAKING SODA	2 ML
¼ TSP	SALT	1 ML
¾ CUP	GRANULATED SUGAR	175 ML
½ CUP	CANOLA OIL	125 ML
2	LARGE EGGS	2
1 TBSP	VANILLA	15 ML
½ CUP	SOUR CREAM	125 ML

PREHEAT OVEN TO 350°F (180°C). LINE OR GREASE A 12-CUP
MUFFIN PAN.

IN A BOWL, WHISK TOGETHER FLOUR, BAKING POWDER,
BAKING SODA AND SALT.

IN A LARGE BOWL, WHISK TOGETHER SUGAR AND OIL
UNTIL SMOOTH. ADD EGGS ONE AT A TIME AND WHISK
WELL AFTER EACH ADDITION. WHISK IN VANILLA. STIR IN
HALF OF THE FLOUR MIXTURE. ADD SOUR CREAM AND
STIR TO COMBINE. STIR IN REMAINING FLOUR MIXTURE
UNTIL JUST COMBINED.

DIVIDE BATTER AMONG PREPARED MUFFIN PANS. BAKE FOR ABOUT 15 MINUTES OR UNTIL TESTER INSERTED IN CENTER COMES OUT CLEAN. LET COOL BEFORE FROSTING. SERVES 12.

LEMON POPPY SEED VARIATION: REDUCE VANILLA TO 1 TSP (5 ML) AND ADD $1\frac{1}{2}$ TSP (7 ML) GRATED LEMON ZEST AND 1 TBSP (15 ML) POPPY SEEDS TO THE BATTER.

VANILLA CREAM CHEESE FROSTING

$\frac{1}{2}$ CUP	CREAM CHEESE, SOFTENED	125 ML
3 TBSP	BUTTER, SOFTENED	45 ML
1 TBSP	VANILLA	15 ML
2 CUPS	POWDERED (ICING) SUGAR	500 ML

IN A BOWL, USING AN ELECTRIC MIXER, BEAT CREAM CHEESE, BUTTER AND VANILLA UNTIL FLUFFY. GRADUALLY MIX IN SUGAR; CONTINUE MIXING FOR ABOUT 5 MINUTES OR UNTIL FLUFFY. SPREAD OR PIPE ICING OVER TOPS OF CUPCAKES.

FUDGY COCOA BROWNIES

IF YOU ENJOY A RICH AND DENSE BROWNIE, THEN YOU'RE GOING TO LOVE THESE. THE INSTANT COFFEE POWDER ENHANCES THE FLAVOR OF THE CHOCOLATE.

3/4 CUP	ALL-PURPOSE FLOUR	175 ML
3/4 CUP	UNSWEETENED COCOA POWDER	175 ML
I TSP	INSTANT COFFEE GRANULES	5 ML
1/2 TSP	SALT	2 ML
3/4 CUP	BUTTER	175 ML
1 1/4 CUPS	GRANULATED SUGAR	300 ML
I TSP	VANILLA	5 ML
3	LARGE EGGS	3
1/2 CUP	CHOCOLATE CHIPS (OPTIONAL)	125 ML

PREHEAT OVEN TO 350°F (180°F). LINE AN 8-INCH (20 CM) SQUARE BAKING PAN WITH PARCHMENT PAPER AND LIGHTLY SPRAY WITH COOKING SPRAY; SET ASIDE.

IN A MEDIUM BOWL, WHISK TOGETHER FLOUR, COCOA, COFFEE GRANULES AND SALT; SET ASIDE. IN A MEDIUM POT, OVER LOW HEAT, MELT BUTTER, THEN ADD SUGAR. COOK, STIRRING OCCASIONALLY, UNTIL MIXTURE IS SMOOTH, ABOUT 3 MINUTES; REMOVE FROM HEAT AND LET COOL 5 MINUTES. ADD VANILLA, THEN EGGS, ONE AT A TIME, STIRRING VIGOROUSLY AFTER EACH ADDITION. STIR IN FLOUR MIXTURE AND CHOCOLATE CHIPS (IF USING), UNTIL JUST COMBINED. SPREAD INTO PREPARED PAN.

BAKE FOR 25 TO 30 MINUTES, UNTIL JUST SET AND EDGES ARE STARTING TO PULL AWAY FROM THE SIDES OF THE PAN. A TESTER INSERTED IN THE CENTER SHOULD COME OUT WITH MOIST CRUMBS ATTACHED. SET PAN ON A COOLING RACK TO COOL. MAKES 16 SQUARES.

TIP: THE BROWNIES CAN BE STORED IN AN AIRTIGHT CONTAINER AT ROOM TEMPERATURE FOR UP TO 4 DAYS OR IN THE FREEZER FOR UP TO 1 MONTH.

TIP: ENJOY THESE BROWNIES IN OUR RECIPE FOR TOFFEE BROWNIE TRIFLE WITH HOT FUDGE SAUCE (PAGE 238).

WHENEVER MY SPOUSE PACKS ME
A SALAD FOR LUNCH, ALL I WANNA
KNOW IS WHAT I DID WRONG.

GINGERBREAD CAKE

*THIS HEAVENLY LIGHT CAKE IS A FAVORITE
ANY TIME OF THE YEAR BUT ESPECIALLY
DURING FALL AND WINTER MONTHS.*

2 CUPS	ALL-PURPOSE FLOUR	500 ML
1 TSP	BAKING SODA	5 ML
1 TSP	GROUND CINNAMON	5 ML
1 TSP	GROUND GINGER	5 ML
1/4 TSP	GROUND CLOVES	1 ML
PINCH	SALT	PINCH
1/2 CUP	BUTTER, SOFTENED	125 ML
2/3 CUP	PACKED BROWN SUGAR	150 ML
1	LARGE EGG	1
3/4 CUP	LIGHT (FANCY) MOLASSES	175 ML
3/4 CUP	HOT WATER	175 ML
	VANILLA ICE CREAM (OPTIONAL)	

PREHEAT OVEN TO 350°F (180°C). LINE A 9-INCH (23 CM)
ROUND CAKE PAN WITH PARCHMENT PAPER.

IN A BOWL, WHISK TOGETHER FLOUR, BAKING SODA,
CINNAMON, GINGER, CLOVES AND SALT; SET ASIDE.

IN A LARGE BOWL, BEAT BUTTER AND BROWN SUGAR
UNTIL FLUFFY. BEAT IN EGG. POUR IN MOLASSES AND
BEAT UNTIL COMBINED. STIR IN HALF OF THE FLOUR, ALL
OF THE WATER, THEN REMAINING FLOUR MIXTURE UNTIL
WELL INCORPORATED. POUR BATTER INTO PREPARED

BAKING PAN. BAKE FOR ABOUT 30 MINUTES OR UNTIL TESTER INSERTED IN CENTER COMES OUT CLEAN. LET COOL IN PAN.

SERVE WEDGES OF CAKE WITH ICE CREAM IF DESIRED. SERVES 8 TO 10.

GLUTEN-FREE OPTION: SUBSTITUTE GLUTEN-FREE FLOUR WITH XANTHAN GUM FOR THE ALL-PURPOSE FLOUR AND BE SURE OTHER INGREDIENTS ARE GLUTEN-FREE. CHECK THE LABELS.

WHY DID THE STUDENTS
EAT THEIR HOMEWORK?
BECAUSE THE TEACHER SAID
THAT IT WAS A PIECE OF CAKE.

DELUXE HAZELNUT SHORTBREAD BARS

*THE SWEETNESS OF RASPBERRY JAM
AND TOASTED HAZELNUTS COMBINED WITH
THE TRADITIONAL BUTTERY FLAVOR OF
SHORTBREAD MAKES THESE BARS DELUXE.*

I CUP	HAZELNUTS	250 ML
I CUP	BUTTER, SOFTENED	250 ML
2 TSP	VANILLA	IO ML
2 CUPS	ALL-PURPOSE FLOUR	500 ML
1/2 CUP	POWDERED (ICING) SUGAR	125 ML
PINCH	SALT	PINCH
I CUP	SEEDLESS RASPBERRY JAM	250 ML

PREHEAT OVEN TO 350°F (180°C). LINE A 13- BY 9-INCH (33 BY 23 CM) BAKING PAN WITH PARCHMENT PAPER; SET ASIDE. SET ASIDE A BAKING SHEET.

PLACE HAZELNUTS ON BAKING SHEET AND TOAST FOR ABOUT IO MINUTES OR UNTIL FRAGRANT. (DO NOT REMOVE SKINS.) CHOP FINELY IN FOOD PROCESSOR OR BY HAND; SET ASIDE.

IN A LARGE BOWL, BEAT BUTTER UNTIL LIGHT AND FLUFFY; BEAT IN VANILLA. IN ANOTHER BOWL, STIR TOGETHER FLOUR, CHOPPED HAZELNUTS, SUGAR AND SALT. BEAT IN FLOUR MIXTURE HALF AT A TIME UNTIL CRUMBLY DOUGH FORMS AND CLUMPS WHEN SQUEEZED. RESERVE I CUP (250 ML) FOR THE TOPPING.

PRESS REMAINING DOUGH IN PREPARED PAN. SPREAD RASPBERRY JAM OVER CRUST AND SPRINKLE WITH RESERVED DOUGH.

BAKE FOR ABOUT 30 MINUTES OR UNTIL TOP IS SET AND EDGES ARE GOLDEN BROWN. LET COOL COMPLETELY IN PAN ON RACK. CUT INTO BARS. MAKES ABOUT 32 BARS.

FREEZER FRIENDLY: CUT INTO BARS AND PLACE IN AIRTIGHT CONTAINER FOR UP TO 1 MONTH.

TIP: FOR A LESS SWEET FILLING, SUBSTITUTE OUR RASPBERRY CHIA JAM (PAGE 32) FOR THE STORE-BOUGHT JAM.

SAYING "SUPER-SIZE IT" AT
CURBSIDE PICKUP DOESN'T WORK
WHEN IT'S THE LIQUOR STORE.

HOMEMADE PEANUT BUTTER SHELL

KIDS OF ALL AGES FIND IT VERY SATISFYING TO CRACK THIS PEANUT BUTTER SHELL, ALMOST AS MUCH AS THEY LOVE EATING THE SWEET TREAT. SIMPLY DRIZZLE OVER ICE CREAM AND WATCH THE SHELL HARDEN.

2/3 CUP	SMOOTH OR CRUNCHY PEANUT BUTTER	150 ML
1/3 CUP	COCONUT OIL	75 ML
2 TBSP	POWDERED (ICING) SUGAR	30 ML
1/8 TSP	SALT	0.5 ML

IN A SMALL SAUCEPAN, OVER MEDIUM-LOW HEAT, STIR TOGETHER PEANUT BUTTER, OIL, SUGAR AND SALT. CONTINUE STIRRING UNTIL COMBINED AND SUGAR IS DISSOLVED, ABOUT 2 TO 3 MINUTES. REMOVE FROM HEAT AND LET COOL SLIGHTLY. TO SERVE, POUR OVER YOUR FAVORITE ICE CREAM AND WAIT A FEW MINUTES TO LET IT HARDEN. MAKES 1 CUP (250 ML).

TIP: REFRIGERATE AND STORE ANY LEFTOVERS IN A COVERED HEAT-SAFE JAR FOR UP TO 1 MONTH. IT WILL SOLIDIFY; REHEAT BRIEFLY IN THE MICROWAVE OR IN A DOUBLE BOILER UNTIL MELTED.

TIP: ANOTHER OPTION IS TO DIP WHOLE OR SLICED BANANAS IN PEANUT BUTTER MIXTURE, THEN FREEZE ON A PARCHMENT PAPER LINED BAKING SHEET.

TIP: THE MAGIC HAPPENS BEST IF YOU USE ICE CREAM STRAIGHT FROM THE FREEZER.

JILLIAN'S COCONUT PANNA COTTA WITH RASPBERRY CHIA JAM

SYLVIA'S DAUGHTER, JILLIAN, CANNOT EAT DAIRY, SO THIS DESSERT IS ONE OF HER FAVORITES SINCE IT USES COCONUT MILK AND ALMOND MILK. EACH DREAMY SERVING HAS A DELICIOUS JEWEL-TONE SPOONFUL OF RASPBERRY CHIA JAM IN THE BOTTOM — YUM!

3/4 CUP	RASPBERRY CHIA JAM (SEE PAGE 32)	175 ML
2 TBSP	WATER	30 ML
1 TBSP	UNFLAVORED GELATIN POWDER (1 ENVELOPE)	15 ML
1 1/4 CUPS	ALMOND MILK	300 ML
1	CAN (14 OZ/400 ML) COCONUT MILK	1
1/4 CUP	LIQUID HONEY	60 ML

SET ASIDE EIGHT 1/2-CUP (125 ML) RAMEKINS OR CUSTARD CUPS; SPOON 1 TBSP (15 ML) RASPBERRY CHIA JAM INTO THE BOTTOM OF EACH. IN A SMALL BOWL, ADD WATER AND SPRINKLE WITH GELATIN; LET STAND FOR 5 MINUTES TO SOFTEN. MEANWHILE, IN A MEDIUM SAUCEPAN, OVER MEDIUM-HIGH HEAT, COMBINE ALMOND MILK, COCONUT MILK AND HONEY; BRING TO A SIMMER. REDUCE HEAT TO MEDIUM, ADD GELATIN MIXTURE AND WHISK UNTIL WELL COMBINED AND GELATIN IS DISSOLVED. REMOVE FROM HEAT AND EVENLY DISTRIBUTE INTO RAMEKINS. REFRIGERATE FOR 4 HOURS OR OVERNIGHT. SERVES 8.

TIP: SOY, OAT OR RICE MILK CAN BE SUBSTITUTED FOR THE ALMOND MILK.

LONDON FOG RICE PUDDING

A LONDON FOG TEA LATTE IS MADE BY COMBINING SWEETENED EARL GREY TEA WITH STEAMED MILK AND VANILLA. INSPIRED BY THIS DELICIOUS HOT DRINK, WE DECIDED TO RECREATE THE FLAVOR IN A RICE PUDDING. THIS CREAMY, RICH, BUT NOT-TOO-SWEET PUDDING IS COOKED IN AN INSTANT POT.

I CUP	ARBORIO RICE, RINSED AND DRAINED	250 ML
2¼ CUPS	STRONG BREWED EARL GREY TEA (4 TEA BAGS)	550 ML
¼ TSP	SALT	I ML
I½ CUPS	HALF AND HALF (10%) CREAM	375 ML
2	LARGE EGGS	2
6 TBSP	GRANULATED SUGAR	90 ML
½ TSP	GROUND CINNAMON	2 ML
½ TSP	GROUND CARDAMOM	2 ML
I TSP	VANILLA	5 ML

IN A 6-QUART INSTANT POT, COMBINE RICE, TEA AND SALT. LOCK LID; SET PRESSURE RELEASE VALVE TO SEALING. PRESS MANUAL PRESSURE COOK; SET TO HIGH FOR 4 MINUTES. (IT TAKES ABOUT IO MINUTES TO COME TO PRESSURE.) WHEN COOKING FINISHES, LET THE PRESSURE RELEASE NATURALLY FOR IO MINUTES, THEN RELEASE ANY REMAINING STEAM BY MOVING THE PRESSURE RELEASE VALVE TO VENTING.

MEANWHILE, IN A BOWL, WHISK TOGETHER CREAM, EGGS, SUGAR, CINNAMON AND CARDAMOM; SET ASIDE.

PRESS CANCEL, OPEN LID. USING A WHISK, FLUFF UP RICE MIXTURE; THEN, IN A STEADY STREAM, VIGOROUSLY WHISK IN THE CREAM MIXTURE. PRESS SAUTÉ AND COOK THE PUDDING, WHISKING CONSTANTLY, FOR 3 MINUTES; MIXTURE WILL BEGIN TO THICKEN, BUT STILL BE A LITTLE SOUPY. PRESS CANCEL; USING OVEN MITTS, REMOVE THE INNER POT AND STIR IN VANILLA. TRANSFER PUDDING TO A MEDIUM BOWL OR EIGHT INDIVIDUAL SERVING BOWLS. ENJOY WARM OR SLIGHTLY CHILLED. PUDDING WILL CONTINUE TO THICKEN AS IT COOLS. SERVES 8.

TIP: THE PUDDING TEXTURE IS BEST THE DAY IT IS PREPARED, BUT IT CAN BE REFRIGERATED FOR UP TO 2 DAYS IN AN AIRTIGHT CONTAINER. THE RICE WILL CONTINUE TO ABSORB LIQUID AS IT COOLS. STIR IN A LITTLE MILK OR CREAM TO DESIRED CONSISTENCY.

APPLE AND PEAR CRUMBLE PUFF TARTS

THE CRUMBLE ON TOP ADDS SWEETNESS AND TEXTURE TO THE FLAKY PASTRY AND TENDER APPLES AND PEARS. WHAT A PERFECT WAY TO END A MEAL!

TARTS

1/4 CUP	BUTTER	60 ML
2	APPLES, PEELED AND SLICED	2
2	RIPE BUT FIRM PEARS, PEELED AND SLICED	2
1/4 CUP	PACKED BROWN SUGAR	60 ML
1 TSP	GROUND CINNAMON	5 ML
1 TBSP	ALL-PURPOSE FLOUR	15 ML
1	SHEET FROZEN PUFF PASTRY, THAWED	1

CRUMBLE

1/4 CUP	ALL-PURPOSE FLOUR	60 ML
2 TBSP	PACKED BROWN SUGAR	30 ML
2 TBSP	BUTTER, SOFTENED	30 ML

TARTS: IN A NONSTICK SKILLET, OVER MEDIUM HEAT, MELT BUTTER AND COOK APPLES, PEARS, BROWN SUGAR AND CINNAMON, STIRRING FOR ABOUT 8 MINUTES OR UNTIL SOFTENED BUT FIRM. STIR IN FLOUR; COOK, STIRRING FOR 1 MINUTE OR UNTIL THICKENED. SET ASIDE AND LET COOL SLIGHTLY.

PREHEAT OVEN TO 400°F (200°C). LINE A BAKING SHEET WITH PARCHMENT PAPER.

ROLL OUT PUFF PASTRY TO A 10-INCH (25 CM) SQUARE. CUT INTO SIX SQUARES. PLACE ON PREPARED BAKING SHEET. TOP EACH WITH SOME OF THE APPLE AND PEAR MIXTURE.

CRUMBLE: IN A SMALL BOWL, COMBINE FLOUR, BROWN SUGAR AND BUTTER UNTIL CRUMBLY AND SPRINKLE OVER TOP OF FRUIT. BAKE FOR ABOUT 15 MINUTES OR UNTIL PASTRY IS GOLDEN AND PUFFED. LET COOL. SERVES 6.

TIP: YOU CAN SUBSTITUTE ALL PEARS OR APPLES INSTEAD OF THE COMBINATION.

TIP: IF YOU ARE NOT USING SHEETS OF PUFF PASTRY, USE HALF A 14 OZ (400 G) PACKAGE AND ROLL OUT AS IN RECIPE.

SKILLET CHERRY CORNMEAL COBBLER

YOU DON'T HAVE TO WAIT FOR CHERRY SEASON TO ENJOY THIS DESSERT. WE USE FROZEN PITTED CHERRIES BECAUSE WE LOVE HOW IT'S A BIG TIME-SAVER FOR BAKING THIS COZY DESSERT ANY TIME OF THE YEAR. THE CORNMEAL ADDS A WONDERFUL CRUNCH AND FLAVOR TO THE BISCUIT TOPPING.

5 CUPS	PITTED FROZEN SWEET CHERRIES, SLIGHTLY THAWED	1.25 L
1/2 CUP	PACKED BROWN SUGAR	125 ML
2 TBSP	CORNSTARCH	30 ML
2 TBSP	LEMON JUICE	30 ML
1 1/2 TSP	GRATED LEMON ZEST	7 ML
1 1/4 CUPS	ALL-PURPOSE FLOUR	300 ML
1/2 CUP	CORNMEAL	125 ML
1/4 CUP	GRANULATED SUGAR	60 ML
1 1/2 TSP	BAKING POWDER	7 ML
1/2 TSP	SALT	2 ML
1 CUP	COLD BUTTERMILK	250 ML
1/2 CUP	BUTTER, MELTED AND COOLED SLIGHTLY	125 ML

PREHEAT OVEN TO 350°F (180°C). IN A 10-INCH (25 CM) CAST-IRON SKILLET, COMBINE CHERRIES (AND ANY ACCUMULATED JUICES), BROWN SUGAR, CORNSTARCH AND LEMON JUICE. OVER MEDIUM HEAT, BRING CHERRY MIXTURE TO A GENTLE BOIL; COOK 5 MINUTES, STIRRING OCCASIONALLY. REMOVE FROM HEAT AND STIR IN LEMON ZEST.

MEANWHILE, IN MEDIUM BOWL, WHISK TOGETHER FLOUR, CORNMEAL, GRANULATED SUGAR, BAKING POWDER AND SALT; SET ASIDE. IN A SMALL BOWL, STIR TOGETHER BUTTERMILK AND BUTTER; STIR UNTIL SMALL CLUMPS OF BUTTER FORM, THEN POUR OVER FLOUR MIXTURE AND STIR UNTIL JUST COMBINED. USE A LARGE SPOON OR ICE CREAM SCOOP TO DROP BATTER OVER FILLING, LEAVE A LITTLE SPACE BETWEEN SCOOPS TO ALLOW DOUGH TO SPREAD DURING BAKING.

BAKE 40 MINUTES, OR UNTIL TOP IS GOLDEN BROWN AND CRISP AND CHERRY JUICES ARE BUBBLING THROUGH. LET COOL 10 MINUTES BEFORE SERVING WITH VANILLA ICE CREAM OR WHIPPED CREAM. SERVES 8.

TIP: BE SURE TO ZEST THE LEMON BEFORE JUICING.

PEANUT BUTTER CARAMEL PRETZEL BARS

WITH THE CARAMEL TOPPING, THESE ARE GOOEY, MESSY AND DELICIOUS BARS YOU WILL WANT TO SHARE. FOR SOMETHING SIMPLER, JUST USE MELTED CHOCOLATE TO TOP YOUR CHOCOLATE PEANUT BUTTER FIX.

PEANUT BUTTER PRETZEL LAYER

1 CUP	CRUNCHY PEANUT BUTTER	250 ML
1/2 CUP	BUTTER, SOFTENED	125 ML
2/3 CUP	POWDERED (ICING) SUGAR	150 ML
1 TSP	VANILLA	5 ML
2 1/2 CUPS	FINELY CRUSHED PRETZELS (SEE TIP)	625 ML

CARAMEL TOPPING

1	BAG (269 G) CARAMELS	1
1/3 CUP	HEAVY OR WHIPPING (35%) CREAM	75 ML
1/2 CUP	COARSELY CRUSHED PRETZELS (SEE TIP)	125 ML
1/2 CUP	SEMISWEET CHOCOLATE CHIPS	125 ML

GREASE OR LINE WITH PARCHMENT PAPER AN 8- OR 9-INCH (20 OR 23 CM) SQUARE BAKING PAN; SET ASIDE.

PEANUT BUTTER PRETZEL LAYER: IN A BOWL, BEAT TOGETHER PEANUT BUTTER AND BUTTER. SLOWLY BEAT IN SUGAR AND VANILLA UNTIL SMOOTH. STIR IN PRETZELS UNTIL WELL COMBINED. SCOOP INTO PREPARED BAKING PAN; COVER WITH PLASTIC WRAP AND PRESS DOWN INTO PAN TO FLATTEN EVENLY. REFRIGERATE FOR AT LEAST 2 HOURS OR UNTIL FIRM.

CARAMEL TOPPING: IN A MICROWAVE-SAFE BOWL, COMBINE CARAMELS AND CREAM. HEAT ON HIGH FOR ABOUT 1 MINUTE AND STIR. REPEAT IN 30-SECOND INTERVALS UNTIL MELTED AND SMOOTH. SPREAD OVER TOP OF PEANUT BUTTER PRETZEL LAYER AND SPRINKLE WITH CRUSHED PRETZELS AND CHOCOLATE CHIPS. REFRIGERATE FOR AT LEAST 2 HOURS OR UNTIL CARAMEL IS SET. CUT INTO SQUARES TO SERVE. MAKES 16 SQUARES/BARS.

TIP: FOR THE FINELY CRUSHED PRETZELS, BE SURE TO USE YOUR FOOD PROCESSOR. YOU SHOULD HAVE VERY SMALL PIECES OF PRETZELS WITH POWDERY FINE PRETZEL PIECES.

FOR THE COARSELY CRUSHED PRETZELS ON THE TOP, YOU CAN SIMPLY BREAK THOSE UP BY HAND.

CHOCOLATE-TOPPED VARIATION: LOOKING FOR A CHOCOLATE TOPPING INSTEAD OF THE CARAMEL TOPPING? OMIT CARAMEL AND MELT $3/4$ CUP (175 ML) OF SEMISWEET CHOCOLATE CHIPS, POUR OVER TOP AND SMOOTH TO COVER. SPRINKLE WITH COARSELY CRUSHED PRETZELS AND REFRIGERATE UNTIL JUST SET. SCORE TOP INTO BARS AND RETURN TO REFRIGERATOR UNTIL FIRM. CUT INTO BARS TO SERVE.

TIP: NEED MORE SWEETNESS FOR THE CHOCOLATE-TOPPED VARIATION? SPRINKLE $1/4$ CUP (60 ML) TOFFEE BITS OVER TOP OF THE CHOCOLATE AND PRETZELS BEFORE REFRIGERATING.

BERRY WHIP

EMILY'S FRIEND DONNA COULD NOT KEEP HER SON AWAY FROM THIS DESSERT. NOW IT'S GOING ON REPEAT AT HER HOUSE SO THE WHOLE FAMILY CAN ENJOY IT!

2 CUPS	FROZEN MIXED BERRIES	500 ML
1/4 CUP	ORANGE JUICE	60 ML
2 TBSP	MAPLE SYRUP	30 ML
1 TBSP	CORNSTARCH	15 ML
1 TBSP	WATER	15 ML
1 CUP	HEAVY OR WHIPPING (35%) CREAM	250 ML
2 TBSP	POWDERED (ICING) SUGAR	30 ML
1 TSP	VANILLA	5 ML

IN A SAUCEPAN, BRING BERRIES, ORANGE JUICE AND MAPLE SYRUP TO A SIMMER. COOK, STIRRING OCCASIONALLY FOR ABOUT 3 MINUTES OR UNTIL SOFTENED. IN A SMALL BOWL, WHISK TOGETHER CORNSTARCH AND WATER. STIR INTO BERRIES AND COOK FOR 1 MINUTE OR UNTIL THICKENED. POUR INTO A BOWL AND REFRIGERATE FOR ABOUT 1 HOUR OR UNTIL COLD.

MEANWHILE, IN A BOWL, USING AN ELECTRIC MIXER, BEAT CREAM, ICING SUGAR AND VANILLA UNTIL STIFF PEAKS FORM. GENTLY FOLD BERRY MIXTURE UNEVENLY INTO CREAM AND SPOON INTO DESSERT GLASSES OR CUPS. REFRIGERATE UNTIL READY TO SERVE. SERVES 4.

MAKE-AHEAD: COVER AND REFRIGERATE FOR UP TO 2 DAYS.

SEMI-FREDDO BERRY WHIP: FREEZE THE BERRY WHIP AND THEN, WHEN YOU ARE READY TO SERVE, SIMPLY LET IT THAW A BIT, SO IT'S LIKE EATING A SOFT ICE CREAM.

FREEZER STRAWBERRY ICE CREAM CHEESECAKES

THIS SUMMERY DESSERT LOOKS LOVELY IN GLASS JAR. IT'S CREAMY AND DELICIOUS — PERFECT FOR A PICNIC OR A BACKYARD CELEBRATION.

2½ CUPS	SLICED STRAWBERRIES	625 ML
2 TBSP	LEMON JUICE	30 ML
2 TBSP	GRANULATED SUGAR	30 ML
2 CUPS	HEAVY OR WHIPPING (35%) CREAM	500 ML
1	CAN (14 OZ/300 ML) SWEETENED CONDENSED MILK	1
8 OZ	BRICK-STYLE CREAM CHEESE, SOFTENED	250 G
½ TSP	VANILLA	2 ML
PINCH	SALT	PINCH
4	GRAHAM CRACKERS, BROKEN INTO SMALL PIECES	4

IN A SMALL POT, OVER MEDIUM HEAT, ADD STRAWBERRIES, LEMON JUICE AND SUGAR; COOK, STIRRING OCCASIONALLY, FOR 8 MINUTES. SLIGHTLY MASH FRUIT AND SET ASIDE TO COOL TO ROOM TEMPERATURE.

MEANWHILE, IN A BOWL, WHIP CREAM; SET ASIDE. IN A LARGE BOWL, USING AN ELECTRIC MIXER, COMBINE CONDENSED MILK, CREAM CHEESE, VANILLA AND SALT UNTIL SMOOTH. FOLD IN WHIPPED CREAM UNTIL JUST COMBINED. FOLD IN STRAWBERRIES AND CRACKERS, LEAVING LARGE STREAKS OF STRAWBERRY VISIBLE.

DIVIDE MIXTURE INTO EIGHT 1-CUP (250 ML) FREEZER-SAFE JARS, FILLING TO ABOUT THREE-QUARTERS FULL. COVER EACH JAR, THEN FREEZE FOR 8 HOURS OR OVERNIGHT. LET SIT AT ROOM TEMPERATURE A FEW MINUTES TO ALLOW THE DESSERT TO SOFTEN SLIGHTLY BEFORE SERVING. SERVES 8.

TIP: A SINGLE GRAHAM CRACKER IS ONE FULL-SIZE RECTANGLE PIECE WITH THE PERFORATIONS INTACT.

TIP: THE STRAWBERRY SAUCE CAN BE PREPARED AND CHILLED OVERNIGHT.

TIP: USE WIDE-MOUTH JARS FOR EASIER FILLING. IF YOU DON'T HAVE MASON JARS, USE SIMILAR SIZE FREEZER-SAFE CUSTARD CUPS OR SMALL BOWLS.

TOFFEE BROWNIE TRIFLE

OMG! REALLY I WANT TO MARRY THIS DESSERT! I
NEED THIS IN MY LIFE! THESE ARE JUST SOME OF THE
COMMENTS RECEIVED AFTER TASTING THIS DESSERT.
THERE IS JUST ENOUGH TANG FROM THE YOGURT TO
MAKE THIS DESSERT NOT TOO SWEET, BUT REALLY, THE
SWEET-TOOTH PEOPLE IN THE ROOM WILL LOVE IT.

1	CONTAINER (608 G) TWO-BITE BROWNIES	1
2 CUPS	HEAVY OR WHIPPING (35%) CREAM	500 ML
1/4 CUP	POWDERED (ICING) SUGAR	60 ML
2 TSP	VANILLA	10 ML
1 CUP	VANILLA GREEK YOGURT	250 ML
3/4 CUP	HOT FUDGE SAUCE (SEE RECIPE PAGE 239)	175 ML
1	BAG (200 G) TOFFEE BITS	1

BREAK UP BROWNIES INTO COARSE PIECES TO MAKE
ABOUT 4 CUPS (1 L); SET ASIDE.

IN A LARGE BOWL, USING AN ELECTRIC BEATER, BEAT
CREAM, SUGAR AND VANILLA UNTIL STIFF PEAKS. BEAT
IN YOGURT.

PLACE ABOUT HALF OF THE BROWNIES INTO AN OVAL
CASSEROLE DISH. TOP WITH ONE THIRD OF THE WHIPPED
CREAM MIXTURE AND DRIZZLE WITH ONE THIRD OF THE
HOT FUDGE SAUCE. SPRINKLE WITH 1/2 CUP (125 ML) OF THE
TOFFEE BITS. REPEAT LAYERS ONCE. TOP WITH REMAINING

CREAM, HOT FUDGE SAUCE AND TOFFEE BITS. COVER AND REFRIGERATE FOR AT LEAST 2 HOURS OR UNTIL BROWNIES HAVE SOFTENED. SERVES 10 TO 12.

TIP: YOU CAN SUBSTITUTE OUR FUDGY COCOA BROWNIES ON PAGE 218 FOR THE TWO-BITES BROWNIES.

HOT FUDGE SAUCE

1/3 CUP	GRANULATED SUGAR	75 ML
1/3 CUP	CORN SYRUP	75 ML
1/3 CUP	WATER	75 ML
1/2 CUP	HEAVY OR WHIPPING (35%) CREAM	125 ML
1 1/4 CUPS	SEMISWEET CHOCOLATE CHIPS	300 ML

IN A SAUCEPAN, BRING SUGAR, CORN SYRUP AND WATER TO BOIL. WHISK IN CREAM AND COOK FOR 1 MINUTE. REMOVE FROM HEAT AND ADD CHOCOLATE. WHISK UNTIL SMOOTH AND LET COOL SLIGHTLY. MAKES ABOUT 1 3/4 CUPS (425 ML).

MAKE-AHEAD: COVER AND REFRIGERATE FOR UP TO 1 WEEK. WARM GENTLY BEFORE USING IN A SMALL SAUCEPAN OVER LOW HEAT OR IN MICROWAVE.

Library and Archives Canada Cataloguing in Publication

Title: Best of Bridge kitchen simple : 125 quick & easy recipes.

Other titles: Kitchen simple

Names: Richards, Emily, author. | Kong, Sylvia, author.

Description: Written by Emily Richards and Sylvia Kong. | Includes index.

Identifiers: Canadiana 20210179716 | ISBN 9780778806820 (hardcover)

Subjects: LCSH: Quick and easy cooking. | LCGFT: Cookbooks.

Classification: LCC TX833.5 .R54 2021 | DDC 641.5/55—dc23

INDEX

C

S